# SUSTAINABLE FASHION
Responsible Consumption, Design, Fabrics, and Materials

by Wearme Fashion

**PROMOPRESS**

**Hoaki Books, S.L.**
C/ Ausiàs March, 128
08013 Barcelona, Spain
T. 0034 935 952 283
F. 0034 932 654 883
info@hoaki.com
www.hoaki.com
hoaki_books

*Sustainable Fashion: Responsible Consumption, Design, Fabrics, and Materials* by Wearme Fashion

ISBN: 978-84-17412-79-1

Copyright © 2021 Promopress, Hoaki Books, S.L.

Proofreading: Mariotti Translations
Cover design: Claudia Martínez Alonso

All rights reserved. The total or partial reproduction of this book, its transmission in any form or by any means or procedure, whether electronic or mechanical, including photocopying, recording or incorporation into an electronic storage and retrieval system, and the distribution of copies of the work through rental or public lending are not permitted without prior authorisation from the publisher.

D.L.: B 19896-2020
Printed in China

# ACKNOWLEDGEMENTS

My dearest team member and Milanese friend, Sara Volpi, who has been with WEARME FASHION almost from day one, her first-hand reviews of created content, supportive research and friendly opinion sharing chats were not taken for granted and are part of this book.

This publication wouldn't have a cohesive visual content without my dearest Italian photographer, Ciro Cennamo, who created those impressive stylish shots you saw. I hope you all agree the clean photography style is awesome.

Creativity is a big portion of this book, so, last but not least, a big hug goes out to Madeline Stone for the amazing graphical work she has done during the transition phase from magazine to book. We all know what it takes to change, it was question of trial and error, exactly like in life and, as we showed you with this book, also in fashion. Eventually we found the most suitable way to present valuable knowledge for you to imbibe, so enjoy reading this book and pass it on when you are ready! Many thanks for the trust, support and will to spread awareness of the precious team behind this creative journey! A sudden meeting with a Promopress publisher at Première Vision has changed my entire 2019, for better and professional growth! It's been a great chance to share a real passion and a true personal love with other people that want to invest in a positive change.

Thanks for all the 50 interviews with people I known or have come to know. All those interviews in person, via Skype, phone, and email were all equally and unequivocally valuable. One by one they were adding, clarifying and extending a wealth of knowledge that converged in single interviews and throughout all the chapters of this book.

# CONTENTS

Introduction .................................................................. 6

**1. Society and Fashion** ............................................. 8
   A View from the Past and the Present ................... 8
   Sustainable Culture ............................................. 12
   The Power of Awareness ..................................... 16
   The Role of Innovation ........................................ 24

**2. Responsible Consumption** ................................. 28
   Responsibilities in Circular Business Models ......... 28
   Upcycling: Myar ................................................. 29
   Reduce, Reuse, Recycle, Repair ............................ 32
   CASE STUDY: Filippa K Not That Complicated Campaign ..... 36
   Wardrobe Digitalization ...................................... 42
   Lease Concept .................................................... 43

**3. Sustainable Design and Style** ............................. 46
   Knitwear ............................................................ 52
   Swimwear .......................................................... 53
   Sensual Tech ...................................................... 54
   Footwear ............................................................ 55
   Streetwear .......................................................... 58
   Craftsmanship .................................................... 60
   Block Print ......................................................... 62
   Made to Order .................................................... 64
   Upcycling .......................................................... 68
   The Role of Colour in Fashion Design ................... 70

**4. Fabrics and Materials** ............................................................. 75
    Global Fibre Consumption ................................................. 76
    Cotton ............................................................................. 77
    Innovation from the Past .................................................... 82
    A Cotton Shirt with a Modern Twist ................................... 88
    Kapok .............................................................................. 94
    Natural Fibres ................................................................. 101
    Viscose, Modal, Tencel ................................................... 105
    Recycled Denim .............................................................. 110
    Case Study: Panama Trimmings-Labels ............................ 118
    Linen .............................................................................. 122
    Wool ............................................................................... 134
    Silk ................................................................................. 140
    Alternatives to Leather .................................................... 146
    A New Kind of Leather Textile ........................................ 154

**5. Synthetic Fibres** ..................................................................... 160
    Microplastics ................................................................... 160

    Afterword ........................................................................ 168
    List of Contributors ......................................................... 168

# INTRODUCTION

The world is connected by the circular law of nature, constantly changing in all tangible aspects of life, from economic projection, industry, personal lifestyle to people's values and interest in fashion. Yet this constant evolution belongs to human nature. Even a temporary stagnation is part of the process' readiness, expecting a lead to take charge. Examples of such expectations are seen in many countries, industries and personal lives. Scandals and unmanaged events stimulated by diverse stagnations are disruptors for existing environments, like in the Italian city of Venice, known as the "City of Water", which has been damaged over the years by record floods. Some regions in India and China are suffering from groundwater infiltration as a result of improper management and outdated industrial processes, ejecting chemicals that have poisoned them or made the situation worse.

Therefore, all changes relate to humanity. To change the current course of events, time is needed to innovate and drive change in all aspects of life, and fashion is certainly no exception. The fashion system and its procedures are changing rapidly thanks to the visionary mindset of innovators, their business perspectives, the renewal of industrial processes and a reconsideration of existing values. In a series of interviews carried out with active representatives of the sustainable fashion market, they spotlight and give insight on how they are integrating basic sustainable principles to create new meaning and values in a new generation of fashion products. A creative world must take its roots from culture, design, innovative ideas, and sustainable materials. If these steps are underestimated in the circular process from a user integration perspective, it can be fatal for the entire system and the laws of nature.

Are you a customer, designer or someone with an interest in the latest shifts of fashion for a better future? Then this book is a valuable asset with first-hand stories allowing you to understand the transition towards a more sustainable fashion.

Photo: Stefano Lupicano

# 1. SOCIETY AND FASHION

## A VIEW FROM THE PAST AND THE PRESENT

We use fashion every day, without even thinking about where it will end up. We want a change. We want to be fashionable. Anna Gallucci Colling, a tutor at the University of Kent, has taught Fashion and Design to students from around the world. She has seen how our perception of and connection with fashion has changed from a long-term relationship to a short-term fling. Going back half a century, when Colling was a little girl, clothing was a luxury. It was treasured and worn for life's best moments, she recalls. People didn't have enough money to buy clothes all the time, and the act of purchasing a new item was seen as an investment. Adding something new to the closet was seen more as an occasional opportunity.

A time in which shops were far and few in between, with a limited selection of styles, the academic suggests that we should find value in our garments as we did in the past, when there were no big chains and people shopped in smaller stores instead. The familiarity that comes with small communities allowed people to pay for garments with credit, little by little. Colling recalls saving up to fulfil the dream of buying a truly desired garment. This approach created a sense of appreciation for owning things, which is almost lost on us nowadays.

Smaller shops and made-to-measure tailoring services were part of society and culture in smaller Italian communities. Tailoring businesses were present in every village, designing garments for longevity, Colling remembers. These businesses made enough money by producing quality, handmade garments that were made to suit one person's body and style, in smaller quantities.

In the late seventies, Colling wasn't aware of big fashion names like Christian Dior, Versace, or Armani, nor did she know what they represented in the fashion world. Although Colling and her peers lived in a village, they still engaged with the fashion through magazines and catalogues. A single copy of a magazine was passed on within a community for inspiration. Some catalogues were available at the library, while others were distributed free of charge, encouraging readers to buy promoted items, though they weren't accessible with everyone's budget. Colling and her peers used to copy the new fashion trends they saw in those sources, while opting for cheaper recreations. Tailors had to realize fashion dreams for inexpensive prices. Besides this, the local tailor served as a tutor to the younger generation. When girls and boys got to a certain age, they attended a tailoring course to learn the basic skills: how to stitch, cut, and make a pattern. This tradition provided Colling's generation with the ability to sew a garment all on their own.

The quality of the clothes allowed people to wear them for a longer time, until they became unwearable. The old items were recycled in exchange for smaller gifts – a doll Colling wanted or glasses she needed for the home. The rag collector would then sell the garments to companies that needed raw materials to recycle into new products, like paper for instance. The old clothes were much more in demand then, since there weren't so many of them available. Much has changed since then, thanks in part to improvements in mass production and a shift in our consumption habits as a society. Tailoring services have almost disappeared in some parts of the world, since not everyone can afford to pay them. Mass production has successfully filled this niche, giving society an easy way to buy affordable clothes with a shorter lifespan. But what we have gained in convenience, we have lost in value and respect.

"I do believe that there has to be a society that buys with consciousness, rather than one that buys garments to wear a couple of times, or even gets rid of clothing that has never been worn", Colling says. Obviously, we have an endless array of choices and the freedom to wear what we like, while the choices in the past were more restricted in terms of expressing individuality. Colling appreciated every item in her wardrobe, "because I had to work for it", she says. Fashion, as a reflection of culture, carefully shapes the individual's style to fit into the surrounding society, indicating who you are and where you belong. Garments can easily express mood and feeling; they can make you confident, sad, or happy, because they are a part of our daily life, and we create memories of life's most important moments while wearing them. The wedding dress, for example, can reveal memories of happy moments shared with the people we love. Colling's story proves that the fewer chances we have to throw garments away, the more carefully we treasure them. This is especially true due to economic and social inequalities. Wealthier societies have become accustomed to parting ways with clothing more easily. In this way, we have lost respect for fashion, while poorer countries don't have the freedom to buy and waste. To move away from a throw-away society, we should look at the past and rediscover the appreciation for garments and the value of individuality, for starters. If we just change consumption habits together, we can change the world.

## AWARENESS

Primarily to build consciousness about what we buy for pleasure, rather than out of greed, and with the intention of making it last. Generally speaking, consciousness can have a different meaning for each individual. One might be very precise in making choices for food and health, but not be aware of the side effect of an unconscious approach towards fashion. On the other hand, others have taken more responsibility for their spending choices and the impact those decisions can have on their environment. "We all should know what fashion is about because we wear it every day", Colling adds.

## TIMELESSNESS

Appreciation for fashion starts with owning something personal that can showcase someone's individuality. The art collector attitude would help select a highly desired garment, not just a fashionable item for one day. Careful thought before purchasing will help reduce waste. Ask yourself these questions before you get in line at the cash register: "Will I wear it?" "Is it going to last?" "Is it going to make me feel good?" "Is it going to give me confidence?" Invest in high quality and comfortable items that get along with your soul.

## BOUTIQUES

Allow the public to experience the touch of a fabric and to understand their taste – what they'd want to wear next. The vendors maintain a social connection with customers, giving advice on suited styles and knowing their preferences in advance. This business model might not be modern or more efficient than online sales, but smaller boutiques still have the value of social interaction and personal relationships that can't be found online.

## RECYCLING

Every country and society have their own way of thinking about recycling and upcycling methods. In the past, for example, used garments were passed down to younger family members or to people in need. Again, not everyone might feel comfortable wearing garments worn by somebody else today, but more advanced recycling methods are being developed every day and will be showcased in this book.

# SUSTAINABLE CULTURE

" The farther back you can look, the farther forward you are likely to see". — Winston Churchill. This famous expression can be applied not only to history and politics, but it holds a fundamental truth for sustainability as well, across diverse cultures. Sustainability can find its roots in traditions, beliefs, knowledge, legends, which can all be helpful for future generations. Societies and cultures, in a globalized sphere, are connected through fashion. Nowadays, there are numerous inspiring examples in textile production and artisanal apparel and footwear, that bring knowledge from the past, celebrating the cultures and traditions of a nation. For centuries, fashion has been perceived differently, especially culturally, due to personal values and beliefs which may or may not be associated with sustainable values. The strongest individual beliefs are what trigger consumer expectations for sustainable fashion. Social and environmental issues connected to the value chain have had an inspirational momentum in the press and digital media recently, renewing customer interest towards sensitive topics like climate change, natural disasters, labour issues, etc.

The Pulse of the Fashion Industry survey has identified 75% of customers across Brazil, USA, China, and the UK consider sustainability an important factor in purchases. If people are confident about the sustainable content of a product, they are more likely to invest in it and pay a premium price. No child labour, no cruelty towards animals, and safe working conditions, are the basics of sustainable values that customers are expecting from businesses. In addition, the survey highlights that responsible sourcing, biodegradable packaging, and recycled materials are among the preferred product features.

On a geographical scale, sustainability varies in meaning and importance; for instance, the social aspect is more considered in the USA, while it is less relevant in China, where environmental concerns are more of an issue. China is still at the beginning of the conversation on sustainability, even if the impact of air and water pollution is no longer headline news. Bringing the conversation down to textiles and customers' decision is a new narrative, explains Heather Kaye, an American designer who has been working in China for over 14 years. Whereas in the US people are well informed about the negative sides of fast fashion, but do not adopt new behaviours fast enough, Chinese customers adapt much faster to changes and new ideas, she says.

Consumer expense is an important driving force for the circular economy's health. The survey shows that current sustainable practices are not a powerful enough driver to switch the buying behaviours of the majority of people. Consequently, the transformation of traditional fashion realities won't happen quick enough without a consumer push. Fashion enterprises have to find alternative solutions to funding, resources, effective collaboration models, and access to innovations, to become successful sustainable industries. Despite global challenges, like the level of economic development, income per capita, and sustainable awareness, the need for government support is crucial in order to resolve double VAT taxation for recycled products in Europe, or for a clothing collection and sorting system. With all these united actions, sustainable culture is shifting from a cool trend towards the mainstream – it's becoming a way of life.

Above all, the trusted communication of a new generation of values is on a brand's shoulders. Brand communication has to find the right angle for addressing customer's needs, product expectations, and the strongest value of sustainability. These steps would support 35% of resistant customers to make a personal transition and change their purchasing behaviours. Creators of sustainable design make every effort to mentor society, businesses and government through educational workshops, pop-ups, or events at local fashion schools, helping to spread environmental awareness and the importance of a circular business model in a narrative that thinks of waste as a valuable

resource. Customers are attracted to an authentic and real story of people behind sustainable and innovative products, as well as transformation in the design process from waste to new materials. On a macro-level, the perception of sustainable products is fluctuating as an important factor in geographies: a company's sustainable achievements, its history, price, eye-catching design or minimalistic style, change depending on geographical and cultural background, explains Marita Setas Ferro, the creative director of Portuguese footwear and accessory brand Marita Moreno.

# THE POWER OF AWARENESS

When it comes to incomprehensible facts or incorrect statements about sustainability, the reliability of that information is called into question; being aware of this and discovering the true facts helps to build trust within society. And when it comes to understanding more about the fashion industry, perhaps the only place to discover this is a museum based in Amsterdam. Fashion for Good is a global platform for sustainable innovation in fashion, which is home to the world's first interactive museum of sustainable fashion. The Fashion for Good Experience encourages visitors of all ages to reimagine purchasing behaviours and empower them through their fashion choices.

## CONSUMER PERSPECTIVE

From interactive themed exhibits – related to product innovations, new textile materials, recycled products, etc. – visitors get a clear idea of the industry's versatility and complexity without needing to be fashion experts. Moving around the exhibition with a radio frequency identity (RFID) bracelet allows visitors to interact with their surroundings, collecting instructions for the various actions they wish to improve in their fashion purchasing behaviours to decrease their impact on the environment. The museum's intention is to show how Good Fashion can be part of your daily life. Visitors can commit to individual actions and earn badges in key categories - consider, choose, use, reuse, activate - that can later be redeemed for a personalized action plan for buying behaviours they can take home.

*Consider:* How visitors think about their clothing needs.
*Choose:* How visitors go about buying and choosing clothes.
*Use:* How visitors care for the clothing they have.

***Reuse:*** How visitors think about an item's next use when they have finished with it.
***Activate:*** How visitors engage with brands, makers and their communities around Good Fashion.

Since its opening in October 2018, 55,000 visitors have come to the Fashion for Good experience, and 45,000 have made commitments towards a Good Fashion Action Plan. Visualizing the existing problems within the industry is helping customers to see the entire picture of the challenges fashion businesses are faded with.

## INDUSTRY PERSPECTIVE

The fashion industry lacks the resources, tools and incentives to put good fashion into practice. One of the most effective ways to change industry practices is to collaborate with innovators, brands, producers, retailers, suppliers, and non-profits organizations. Fashion for Good encourages such collaboration, bringing together a community of like-minded organizations working on sustainable solutions in their co-working space based in Amsterdam. Likewise, the Accelerator and Scaling Programmes seek to find disruptive innovations that can enable the shift towards a circular fashion ecosystem. So far, over 1,500 innovators have been identified, and it is up to the industry to consider if they are to make this change. To bridge the gap between innovation and mainstream implementation, innovative start-ups should be funded. Earl Singh, Marketing specialist at Fashion for Good says, "With the need to change and the abundance of innovation, there are enough incentives for industry stakeholders and investment groups to explore the investment opportunities in this new space". Through effective initiatives and by working collaboratively, the fashion industry can transform into a system that is regenerative by nature, no matter how deeply rooted current practices are.

## RETAIL PERSPECTIVE

For sustainable fashion to become accessible to every consumer, firstly, it must appear on the shelves of every major retail store. We need it in all of those favourite shopping destinations where we regularly go and spend time browsing and choosing the right item for us. Whether it's a department store, shopping mall, or specialized e-shop, most of them still need to join the sustainable offer bandwagon. Several steps must be taken by different players to reverse the state of things, beginning with designers and trade fairs. The German Messe Frankfurt Exhibition responded with its newest trade fair concept Neonyt. The latest event is a contemporary version of its predecessors' Ethical Fashion Show and Green Showroom, which began to shape German culture to perceive sustainable fashion as stylish. Neonyt is carrying on the task, paving the way for responsible creatives to break into Berlin's major retail stores and beyond.

## EVOLUTION OF STYLE

For 10 years, the Green Showroom and Ethical Fashion Show has strived to dispel the cliché that links sustainable fashion with hippie, old school style, like an echo from the past. In the early 1970s, the industry was just beginning to come up with new ideas about possible responsible businesses, overlapping with the beginning of the climate crisis and an increasing lack of natural resources. Although environmental protection was a more familiar concept, its link to sustainable fashion was still being forged. At that time, "even the word 'sustainability' did not exist", recalls Schwenzfeier – Neonyt's exhibition director. At best, he describes "the scenery [as] being kind of eco-styled". In the 70s, this rule-driven style was considered acceptable, but the main problem was that it did not adapt to fit contemporary fashion tastes. "Eco fashion" had nothing to do with fashion as we see it, rather it was more about apparel items with which to cover the body, adding a touch of "feelgood" factor, recalls Schwenzfeier. This served as a starting point for Magdalena Schaffrin, current Creative Director of Neonyt, to establish the first Berlin-based Green Showroom in 2009. Serving as an opportunity to connect sustainability and fashion as a newly blended concept, it highlighted creative designs and introduced them to high-end boutiques, Schwenzfeier says.

Green Showroom – the pioneering platform – immediately caught the attention of Messe Frankfurt, which was looking for solutions in the field of sustainability and textiles. After acquiring and joining forces with Schaffrin, the platform progressed and increased its participants, from 25 labels early on, to 170 in 2019, 65 of which were from Germany. There is no doubt, design and style are the money-making force of fashion. According to this core concept, the Neonyt team is carefully selecting fashion labels to present the best of ethical fashion at each show. To certify its selection criteria – that brands are sustainable and fashionable enough – Schaffrin takes charge on the style side, evaluating the portfolio of potential exhibitors, including lookbooks, visual communications, social media, teams, and production capacity, to ensure all exhibitors are in line with the vision of the show. All this meticulous research and selection is put in place to meet consumer and retailer expectations which are waiting to be inspired by iconic styles without seeing any difference in terms of colour or quality between responsibly produced garments and conventional ones, Schwenzfeier explains. Eco-fashion design should combine garment usability and style inspiration to mirror the commercial success of conventional fashion, while sustainable aspects should be kept in the background to create an emotional "feelgood" effect. Schwenzfeier recognizes that the new positioning of Neonyt – stepping out of the niche of shows called "Ethical" and "Green" – is positively affecting the promotion of eco-fashion through new retail channels. The show attracts way more conventional retailers than in the past, meaning they can positively contribute to spreading sustainable fashion through their extensive retail network and establish a strong relationship with end customers. Neonyt's priority is to attract buyers and conventional retailers to extend the success of sustainable fashion every season and to ensure its growth. Penetrating into Galeries Lafayette in Paris, Selfridges in the UK or Peek & Cloppenburg in Germany, would mean higher visibility for brands and provide an extensive customer base for a greater selection of sustainable styles.

## GERMAN FASHION SCENE AND ITS LABELS

According to Schwenzfeier, German consumption of responsible fashion contributes to 4% of the entire fashion market, covering all segments and categories: menswear, womenswear, footwear, accessories. Berlin now is seen as one of the most sustainable capitals in the world, he adds. And Neonyt has become a major representative of responsible fashion on a global scale. "The fair is becoming increasingly relevant for both exhibitors and retailers", he says, adding that there is no trade show in any other fashion capital, be it London, Paris, Milan or New York, with the same outreach in terms of visitor numbers and the number of fashion labels presented under one roof at any one time.

The platform took years of constant development to win the status of trusted partner, acquire the know-how, and establish networking, in the field of real sustainability. As a result, Neonyt receives much praise within the sector. Even its media presence was recognized by Launch Metrics as having the greatest and most valuable impact of all the trade shows happening during Berlin Fashion Week. Neonyt's strength comes from the collaboration between people who share the same innovative vision: a long-term strategy to push creativity, style and sustainability for a better, prolonged future.

Schwenzfeier has proudly extolled some of the labels in the Neonyt portfolio - **Lanius**, **Degree Clothing**, **Langerchen**, **Recolution**, **Jan n' june**, **Mymarini**, **Lovjoi**, **Puya** - as an example of entrepreneurs pushing product innovation, guaranteeing reliable product content and appetible design. This generation of German fashion labels represents a niche among fashion realities that fits the local lifestyle.

▶ **Lanius**
Credentials: Established in 1999, in Cologne.
A cool brand for the woman of the world. The founder, Claudia Lanius, an eco-fashion pioneer, and her brand are known for their perfect blend of fashion and style, without the slightest hint of sustainable credentials.

▶ **Degree Clothing**
Credentials: Established in 2010, in Augsburg.
Daily wear solutions for the skateboard scene. Connecting with subculture lifestyle to propel fashion awareness into the local younger generation.

▶ **Langerchen**
Credentials: Established in 2013, near Munich and in Shanghai.
Makes apparel for rainy and winter days in a timeless way. Philipp Langer

and his wife Miranda are urban outdoor wear specialists, adding little gimmicks to raincoat, jacket, and trench coat designs.

▶ **Recolution**
Credentials: Established in 2010, in Hamburg.
Streetwear is the modern classic of a basic wardrobe. Relaxed, casual fit is a must-have to keep up with the urban speed of life.

▶ **Jan n' june**
Credentials: Established in 2013, in Hamburg.
Anna and Julia, fashion designers and partners, stick to creating minimalistic and price-oriented women's attire, from attractive coats and blouses to tops and t-shirts. A springboard for saying goodbye to fast fashion.

▶ **Mymarini**
Credentials: Established in 2013, in Hamburg.
Hints of elegance are in the DNA of **Mymarini**'s sporty lifestyle. Surf and swimwear designed to preserve the pure moments of happiness one can experience when in contact with nature. High quality, durable textiles come in double layers, offering a new option for the perfect vacation style.

▶ **Lovjoi**
Credentials: Established in 2014, in Dürmentingen.
Expanding the intimate female wardrobe with lingerie and stockings. Gradually introducing a new assortment of apparel and denim collections to reinforce its position in the eco market.

▶ **Puya**
Credentials: Established in 2008, in Gottfrieding.
Conquers heights when skiing and hiking. Multifunctional outdoor items balancing sustainability, style, and functionality.

**PERSONALIZED PAINT**

1. Jacket: **Fade Out Label**  |  Trousers: **Church of the Hand**  |  Swimsuit: **Nakt**  |  Earring: **Natascha von Hirschhausen**  |  Shoes: **Trippen**

2. Jacket: **Kluntje**  |  Hoodie: **Lana**  |  Skirt: **Natascha von Hirschhausen**  |  Leggings: **Stylist's Own**  Cap: **Church of the Hand**  |  Nose Ring: **Mies Nobis**  |  Shoes: **Nat-2**

3. Jacket + Shirt: **Wunderwerk**  |  Jeans: **Maison Matz**  |  Necktie: **VC**  |  Necklace + Ring: **Mies Nobis**  Ring: **Martin Guthmann**  |  Shoes: **Haferl**

4. Jacket + T-shirt: **Phyne**  |  Trousers: **Maison Matz**  |  Bag: **Pat Guzik**  |  Socks: **Wolford**  |  Shoes: **Velt**

**(UN)TRADITIONAL**

5. Jacket + Trousers: **Allpamamas**  |  Bikini Top: **Phylyda**  |  Bag + Glasses: **Waqar J Khan**  Shoes: **Trippen**

6. Jacket: **Kluntje**  |  Shorts: **Phylyda**  |  Scarf: **Vintage**  |  Earrings: **The Boyscouts**  |  Necklace: **Martin Guthmann**  |  Bracelet: **Trippen**  |  Shoes: **Vintage**

7. Vest: **Kluntje**  |  Trousers: **Schmidttakahashi**  |  Bag: **Humour Noir**  |  Shoes: **Vintage**

8. Shirt: **Waqar J Khan**  |  Vest: **Vintage**  |  Nose Ring: **Mies Nobis**  |  Socks: **Pat Guzik**  |  Shoes: **Haferl**

**DENIM DAZE**

9. Blouse: **Hessnater**  |  Jeans: **Schmidttakahashi**  |  Collar: **Before 7am**  |  Scarf: **Vintage**  Glasses: **Neubau**  |  Ring: **Mies Nobis**  |  Earring: **Informis Studio**  |  Shoes: **Stylist's Own**

10. Jacket: **Mud Jeans**  |  Shirt: **Wunderwerk**  |  Trousers: **Kluntje**  |  Bag: **Ackermann Taschenmanufaktur**  |  Necktie: **VC**  |  Nose Ring: **Mies Nobis**  |  Shoes: **Trippen**

11. Jacket: **Schmidttakahashi**  |  Coat: **Church of the hand**  |  Trousers: **VC**  |  Top + Leggings: **Lana**  Hat: **Pat Guzik**  |  Earrings + Necklace: **Mies Nobis**  |  Shoes: **Trippen**

12. Jacket + Trousers: **Lanius**  |  Top: **Lana**  |  Skirt: **Graciela Huam**  |  Hat: **Spatz**  Glasses: **Neubau**  |  Ring: **Mies Nobis**  |  Shoes: **Stylist's Own**

# PERSONALIZED PAINT

1

2

3

4

# (UN)TRADITIONAL

5

6

7

8

# DENIM DAZE

9

10

11

12

Photo: Neonyt / Messe Frankfurt

# THE ROLE OF INNOVATION

Fashion and technology feed off each other - they work together to constantly evolve and be effective at every stage of the fashion industry. In other words, tech-savvy expertise is fundamental for innovative and sustainable fashion. The potential impact of innovation is like an immense sky for designers, whose credibility is strongly connected to creating fresh, groundbreaking designs. Technology should be easily accessible to creative thinkers in order to develop the fashion industry and make their mark in a comparatively large market.

Thus, a relationship between technology and creativity is crucial, whether it is integrated into the entire business model or just in a single process. Across the product life cycle there are certain factors, like trend forecasting, design, sample production, manufacturing, retailing, and post-sales services, that can radically change the scale and the outcome of a fashion business. Technology also addresses consumption behaviours, paving the way for a more agile, collaborative, and sustainable industry. Ishwari Thopte, a FashTech Officer from the Centre for Fashion Enterprise, predicts that the fashion industry still needs a few more years to become more tech-savvy and acquire the same level of expertise that other industries have reached.

## FASHION TECH LANDSCAPE

Thopte believes that the geographical position of the UK makes it a gateway for Europe and the USA, enabling it to incorporate new technologies much faster than in the rest of Europe. A forward-thinking society can offer much to tech innovation hubs, like those in Silicon Valley. For example, it can help explore the connection between fashion and technology, as the fashion market in the USA is still primarily focused on the commercial and sportswear side of the business, rather than the innovation aspect.

Moreover, she says that London Fashion Week has been known for its innovation, streetwear, and cutting-edge technology for a long time. In 2013, forefront developers used technology in a theatrical way to create and showcase new experiences as part of their fashion shows. During the last couple of years, brands have been more interested in applying technology to the commercial side of the fashion cycle, believing this to be the best way to boost company sales and to create new buying experiences. On the other hand, augmented or virtual reality is being used to showcase their latest collections on the catwalk. Immersive technologies, like augmented reality, allow users to 'see now, buy now,' blurring the lines between the physical and the digital worlds by merging interactive show experiences with real and virtual models. By using a headset, a viewer can change styles, flip through colour options, and even buy their favourite garment right at the show. Augmented reality has become more popular than virtual reality because it merges the artificial and the real, and can be used on mobile phones, whereas virtual reality still requires special headsets for the experience, making it less seamless.

The topic of returns and increase in profitability is another side of e-commerce where technology can help customers make the right decisions before purchasing. In most cases, product returns are due to the wrong fit, a difference in colour, or a difference in style, since customers make shopping decisions based on aesthetic appeal and the way a garment looks on a model, Thopte explains. Now, e-commerce is using artificial intelligence and algorithms to suggest styles to customers that fit their preferences and profiles. Thopte points out that not every business needs to have tech elements to support sales - in fact, technology should be relevant to an existing business model. Once a designer or brand has a great product, by knowing its market niche and customer profile, they can understand if and where to implement technology. A pre-evaluation of consumers final reactions is required, as technology might drive them away if they don't know much about it or prefer human interaction to an interface. Also, smaller players might not have the same budget as the biggest brands, but their size allows them to integrate technology much faster with an agile approach towards innovation.

Consequently, small businesses have different ways to access to technology, whether through collaboration or mutual 'give and take' with other companies, or even by developing skills within the team. In contrast to small players, large enterprises usually scout for innovation outside of their companies to find the most interesting solutions already made available on the market by tech startups. For this purpose, companies like Farfetch have established their own accelerator to support the most interesting fashion tech startups that could be useful to their business. In this situation it is much harder to incorporate change, as larger enterprises require more time and resources, Thopte explains.

All tech startups need support and incubation, which CFE has been providing since 2003. CFE has been helping London-based fashion designers understand the business side of the industry and attain economic growth and stability. Since then, CFE has assisted fashion tech startups with 80% software, 19% hardware, and 1% biotech, focusing on new materials and textiles. Due to the expertise of UK investors in the software market, software startups are highly funded and scaled businesses, making them more attractive to investors.

Hardware and biotech businesses have to overcome the struggle to scale up mainly on their own, as these are considered high-risk businesses. Lack of infrastructure also plays its part as an obstacle to European wearable technology businesses. Since the majority of production happens in China, the solution can also be found there. However, due to different standards in Europe, this path requires quality assurance and precise review on a diverse scale. In addition, new materials and textiles are also hard to stack up unless startups can figure out cost effective production methods and find unlimited supplies of raw materials, Thopte explains.

The wearable tech market is relatively new in Europe. It is creating opportunities to discover new ways of manufacturing and retailing, and opening doors to a growing lifestyle tech market. On a global scale, the USA is leading the wearable tech field, where companies like Apple, Samsung and Fitbit are major suppliers. In their fixed production methodology, they uplift products with new features. Rapid production and access to technology in the Asian market has pushed the wearable tech sector to develop a wide range of lifestyle products in different categories, like bathroom or kitchen appliances, and even makeup, at lower prices.

European customers aren't even aware of high-tech Korean, Japanese, or Chinese products due to the factor of longevity. According to Thopte, UK customers are used to purchasing more durable products, which differentiates the purchasing power of UK customers. The latest European wearable tech products are promoted on wearable tech kickstart or crowdfunding platforms in order to raise funding for the first line of products, and most of them prove to be successful. Thopte admits that without utilising crowdfunding platforms with the right target outreach, it is very hard to recreate the same level of success for the next set of products or to develop a stable business. Digitalization is changing the retail world, so mastering digital marketing tech tools, like SEO, PPC, and viral growth marketing, would help tech startups to acquire the right target audience to become an overnight success.

In the UK, institutions like the Fashion Innovation Agency at the London College of Fashion establish relationships with technology service providers, creating synergies with the fashion designers of tomorrow and fostering innovation. Final year students at this prestigious college are able to experiment with the latest software and hardware technologies in order to explore possibilities for fashion consumption in retail or to innovate the design process, Thopte explains. The benefits of such collaborations are valuable and free. The earlier students are given access to tech resources, the more advanced they can become in this regard. This way, they are more likely to adopt technology at an early stage and build their future businesses with a more innovative and functional approach.

# 2. RESPONSIBLE CONSUMPTION

## RESPONSIBILITIES IN CIRCULAR BUSINESS MODELS

The value of sustainable design that avoids harm to the people's health and natural resources has become an activating element in creating a value-based consumption economy. In the circular economy, the creator of a new generation of products has prime ownership of its designs. From day one, designing with a mindset specifically oriented towards the re-use and disassembly of components has become fundamental to the recreation of future products. This can categorically prevent the spawning a new generation of unrecycled and harmful waste from its activities. Good design requires a sound choice of fabric. By knowing the fabric's composition, harmful substances that were never meant to be in contact with people's skin can be excluded. In such fast-changing times as these, all participants in the circular economy have to be engaged to innovate the design methodology and the value-based consumption model. If customers can't see enough value in modernizing their consumption habits, then manufacturers' or designers' good intentions alone won't shift their ground or make a change.

To produce the finest components and to compete with proper resources, manufacturers should oversee demand and constantly upgrade their manufacturing process. In such a model, the designer works as a creative idea generator, as a bridge between the industrial textile world and the customer base, creating trusted products aligned with the values of its design. A new generation of durable products suggests support of maintenance services in order to minimize waste within the production cycle and at the end of a product's life.

Cradle to Cradle's design philosophy proposes to deal with already accumulated waste material, creatively reusing it in new forms through upcycling concepts. However, the authors of Cradle to Cradle were worried because certain materials can be unsafe since they were not created with this philosophy in mind. The reliability of materials for use in upcycling can be controlled through a complete understanding of their composition. Sustainably made fabrics are considered more ethically transparent and a luxury choice in a world of limited resources. The upcycling concept is mainly used by individual designers who want to sparkle and differentiate themselves in the crowded fashion scene. The commercial success of upcycling on a wide scale has to identify a reliable supply of materials together with authentic design, and eventually propose a price point that works well with brands' individual business models. Despite the fact that the upcycling concept doesn't use new material resources and has a better value for the environment, a smart approach is often needed to reduce the time frame of the re-design process that determines the final price.

## UPCYCLING: MYAR

Numerous examples of fashion designers working in the business confirm that the vintage fashion market is growing and can be profitable. One example for a commercially well-positioned product is based in Italy, where the idea of camouflage was first used by the MYAR brand. Its upcycling model is focused on one typology of product – military wear. In fact, it sources raw materials from unused military stock to form the brand's specialized product category, aligned with themed communication, to inform its global audience. MYAR was born from a divine passion for existing military style, embodying stories of the past hidden in the longevity of military garments. The 40 - 70 year-old uniforms from World War II and military service that have waited a long time to be refashioned and to breathe the air of a new life. For a second, imagine the amount of unused camouflage across Western Europe, Eastern Europe and the USA linked to the origins of war. These resources can dress current and future generations once again. The garments are customized through meticulous sartorial work to refit camouflage from pragmatic military use to urban streetwear. An appealing contemporary look is changing its initial intent from hiding yourself to showing yourself. Reversed inside-out, the tonality of camouflage is either hand-painted or wood stamped with ink, respecting original shapes and typology. Some camouflage is elaborated with mixtures of prints, uniting cultures and typologies of different camouflage with certain categories of military service, climate and geography: Marine Corps, Navy, Air Force, etc. The functional military style has inspired fashion designers at every level. From the shape of jackets or trousers and the colour of camouflage to garment assembly, so that most of the pieces available on the market are all interpretations of military uniforms. Through customization, the founder of MYAR, Andrea Rosso, opens up the knowledge and resources that were used in the past to create long-lasting military garments. Their specific construction, assembly, tailoring and selected textiles are things that cannot be found anymore; such longevity would be impressive and appreciated now. Rosso discovered that intelligent design demands a slow pace, it takes take time to conceptualize and produce; there is no place for haste.

In the past, pure cotton or coated cotton and blended fabrics, like wool and polyester or cotton and polyester, were mainly used for outdoor activities and unpredictable weather conditions. Later, military attire switched from pure cotton to cheaper and more durable polyester, Rosso adds. MYAR conveys the history of a garment through QR codes and a paper guide with a tracked story detailing when and where it was used. The QR code can also track the longevity of a garment as well as changes in owner history. Customers receive customized garments packed with leftovers memorializing the previous life and transformation of the uniform into a contemporary item. MYAR is distributed in Japan, UK, France, Germany and the USA. On the international retail scale, Japanese markets were the first to embrace the brand's vision, showing their curiosity for fashion history and their extensive habit of collecting American second-hand clothes more than anywhere in Europe so far. All these style collectors love vintage and nostalgia as a reminder of history. Rosso admits that many people still can't accept the idea of wearing other people's clothes rather than new ones. Yet, the mentality of people is changing towards used, vintage fashion; "it is selling much more than before", he admits. There are future predictions that 1/3 of every wardrobe will consist of vintage clothes.

Photo: Gavin Watson

# REDUCE, REUSE, RECYCLE, REPAIR

Filippa K's Sustainability Director, Elin Larsson, has been an influential voice in the field of sustainability for the Swedish powerhouse brand for a decade. She was around, in early 2000, when the first seeds of fashion awareness were planted in Sweden by local media outlets that covered issues like wages and working conditions for overseas industry employees. At that time, consumers were becoming interested in looking behind the scenes of how and where their garments were produced and local brands began approaching these issues more seriously.

Among them was Filippa K, a label founded in 1993 with the goal of providing comfortable, practical, yet always stylish basics for men and women. As Larsson states, "in some ways, the customer has pushed the agenda for sustainability within the brand", and it was quick to respond to society's evolving values, committed to listening to its eco-conscious customers early on. "In Sweden, we talk a lot about […] value-based consumption", she explains – the idea that people support those whose values are in line with their own. And today it has become a pattern: local consumers are paying more attention to animal welfare and eco-friendliness, and are expecting more from the brands they love. Larsson feels that, despite all the information available today, local customers still have a hard time comparing what's on the market and determining the most sustainable option on their own. From her perspective, it's not easy to gather insights on the variety of alternatives right now, so people are evaluating brands to the best of their knowledge, basing judgements on what's available on a company's website or in a sustainability report. All fashion labels have a fundamental responsibility to educate their customers on how to make more sustainable choices, Larsson believes. For instance, researchers have proved that the production process of a garment determines its environmental impact, "meaning that the spinning, weaving, and dyeing of a fabric has the biggest impact", rather than the "kind of fibre [it] has been made of", she continues. This means that a T-shirt made of organic cotton doesn't necessarily mean it is sustainable, because it might have been woven, coloured or dyed at a place that uses lots of water, lots of chemicals and fossil fuels and so on. Hopefully, today's technology and digital solutions can help provide trustworthy information about a brand's value chain and allow consumers to track and trace the manufacturing process for every product. In this sense, Filippa K is an example of transparency, communicating certain steps of the production process – from which sewing and cutting factories they work with, to the amount of time they have spent collaborating with a specific company, and so on. As for now, they don't disclose names of the suppliers in the value chain: who has dyed or made the fabric, that's the plan, Larsson says. Though not all customers care for these details, this honest approach creates special connections and opens the door to strong, trusting relationships. Yet, every relationship has its ups and downs. Creative industries are constantly on the lookout for ways to better satisfy the needs of customers. Today, retail is identifying the most attractive, new approaches to improving consumption practices. Larsson describes it as a never-ending journey of trial and error before the brand and its customer fully understand each other and reach the ideal scenario where the expectations of both sides are met.

Fillippa K, for instance, experimented a new approach to help its customers refresh their wardrobes without spending a lot on garments they might only wear a few times. Swedish customers can, in fact, access highly curated rental programs, which offer garments for everyday wear, business events, and special occasions – like weddings, cocktail parties, and New Year's Eve parties. "What we see in Sweden now is […] new companies that offer rentals or subscriptions [to] clothes and position themselves as wholesale stores or retailers that can offer different brands and a bigger range of […] clothes", like leather jackets or business suits, Larsson explains. Although it was worth a try, the experiment did not meet the brand's expectation, that's why Fillippa K is continuing to focus on the primary goal of creating fashion according to a circular business model. Back in 2014, the brand launched a new internal framework called "Circular Fashion", developed around the "four R's": reduce, repair, reuse and recycle.

The four R's address every stage of a garment's creation, guiding the brand on how to move away from a traditional linear business model and towards a circular one.

**Reduce** explores "how to design and produce new garments [to be] as sustainable as possible in the right quantities [...], creating no waste and [making] sure that they are recyclable", Larsson explains. Ensuring every garment is part of a closed-loop system.

**Repair** addresses "how we get the customers to take care of their clothes, so that they [...] last as long as they were meant to", she says. Filippa K achieves this step through its care concept, which promotes garment care methods to its users. According to a report from the Waste and Resources Action Programme – a recycling non-profit advocacy based in the United Kingdom – prolonging the life of a garment by nine months would decrease its environmental impact by 20 to 30 percent. Another recent study showed the impact of user action, or inaction: doubling the lifespan of a garment would decrease its environmental impact by 49 percent.

These are not figures to scoff at, illustrating the value caring for garments properly can have. Because Filippa K clothes are made to stand the test of time, the company makes it a priority to use fabrics of the highest quality. "We've put a lot of effort into finding the right fabric, but also [making] sure that we get the right care instructions for that type of fabric", Larsson explains. When producing sensitive garments from luxury fabrics with special care instructions, the brand adds extra hang tags that spell out how to clean and maintain the garments.

Helping customers keep their garments in good shape also helps Filippa K keep the planet in good shape. The third "R" that the company focuses on is **Reuse**, or ensuring "that all our clothes get the chance to [a] second, third or fourth life through our Collect concept and second hand stores", Larsson says. In 2015, the brand started a garment collecting system where customers can bring in clean, well-maintained Filippa K garments they no longer want in exchange for a 15 percent discount voucher. Through its own Stockholm-based second-hand store, they found an alternative to disposal practices where new users can have access to collected garments.

However, the garments that have had a long, happy life of wear (and tear) have a different destination. The final "R", **Recycle**, asks "how to get overused clothes back to be recycled into new garments or other products", Larsson continues. Recycling clothes is a process the brand is still mastering, though. "Closing material loops in order to minimize [the] textiles [that end] up in landfills or get incinerated is a big challenge which requires new infrastructural solutions", she states. For this reason, the company has teamed up with other actors to confront the challenge, including Re:newcell, the Swedish Chemicals Agency, and the Swedish Environmental Protection Agency, among others.

# CASE STUDY: FILIPPA K NOT THAT COMPLICATED CAMPAIGN

From the brand mission and strategic company perspective, let's move on to a real-life, mindful consumption style practice curated by Filippa K. Back in Fall 2017 the brand launched the Not That Complicated campaign, turning its passion for mindful consumption into a persuasive communication approach, in an attempt to pre-construct a change in consumers' behaviors.

Filippa K has been known for its basic and classic style that is easy to mix and combine. The campaign suggests – as a great starting point – to spend some time and think carefully about which essential garments you might need to have in your wardrobe; those that work best for your lifestyle and can be worn in multiple styling options. Accurately identifying your own personal essentials could mean the success or failure of a well planned basic wardrobe.

Using a series of black and white photographs, the campaign is a step by step guide for women on how to get on track with a mindful consumption, non-verbally stressing how "In today's complex world simplicity is the purest form of luxury". It then visualizes the transformation of an ordinary fashion lifestyle into a wardrobe full of new possibilities, simply by showing multiple styling options that customers can create with just seven essential pieces in their closet. In practice, it is showing how to master styling tricks in order to create 18 different looks.

As a result, Filippa K helps their customers save money and closet space, and cares for the environment by inspiring them to think smarter about their wardrobes and their needs. With the Not That Complicated campaign, the brand is addressing a problem all women have: spontaneous buys that weren't considered properly in terms of styling or use, and that overcrowd closets with unworn clothes.

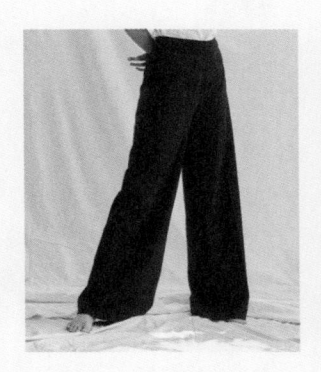

# 7
# garments

# 18 looks

Larsson points to a Swedish study that showed how 70 percent of Swedish consumers wear 50 percent or less of what's in their wardrobe, and 30 percent of consumers are frustrated with their closet. According to her, a well-planned, basic, high-quality wardrobe can do away with overcrowded, but under-used ones; she even thinks that "it's better to have a smaller [wardrobe]".

Filippa K has successfully identified the right communication approach to create a special connection with customers and to translate the brand's basic values. The Not That Complicated campaign has been followed by further campaigns, "Simply Slip Into" and "Easy as That", which continue to inspire a movement of mindful consumption.

Photo: Philip Messman

## OUR INDIVIDUALITY

The Swedish label has also identified four key customer personalities and the relationships they each have with their closets. How we interact with our wardrobe, the way we dress and what drives us to upgrade our style can teach us a lot. According to Larsson, "different users have different speeds of updating their wardrobes". She finds "it's really hard for a brand to affect different wardrobe behaviours", because they are so personal. "In the end we have to accept [the] different kind of behaviours and find a sustainable solution for them", she adds.

# Wardrobe Personalities

### 1. The Changemaker
Those who constantly want to change their style.

This persona is constantly seeking inspiration in fresh, modern styles. They have a deep love for their rich wardrobe, which has an overwhelming selection for any time and any season.

### 2. The Timeless attitude
Those who are very selective when shopping and keep their clothes forever.

These shoppers meticulously curate every new garment before taking the dive and making a purchase. They evaluate their lifestyle and their needs first, and they aim to keep what they buy forever.

**3. The give it a try**

Those who will try anything once.

These people try to wear styles new to them. They adore the look on others, but tend to forget their own lifestyle and aesthetic in the dressing room. Perhaps they never wear skirts, but become convinced that a particular skirt will turn them around. After they bring the new piece home, they find it difficult to integrate it into their style and the new skirt gets hung in the closet to collect dust, waiting for a better moment.

**4. The one treasure**

Those who keep one particular garment forever due to its design and the emotions and memories tied to it.

This person has a favourite piece, one that was most likely expensive and well-made, that they dote on and cherish. They make sure to take excellent care of the garment, since it's irreplaceable, and only wear it on special occasions, so that it maintains its good form.

# WARDROBE DIGITALIZATION

The vitality of a value-based consumption ecosystem depends on stable relationships between the final customer, the designer, and the interdependence of material supply. Every created garment has an effect on both a local and global scale. Within the circular system, such implications are managed by services to support garment maintenance; it's possible re-use or finding a new owner for it in every single country. New service enterprises tackle the existing massive disconnection between products, enhancing visibility for possible future owners. Digital wardrobes and rental programs aim to reduce the side effects of unused existing fashion products, empowering people to optimize a style, and maintain or recycle clothes through renting solutions or by re-selling them.

A digital wardrobe is a relatively new service that still has to overcome a data privacy challenge to function properly in a seamless, easy way. The idea behind the concept is to have a copy of the physical wardrobe in a digital version for better management. A recent change in European data protection legislation has set a high standard to protect personal data, allowing people to decide on which web site to enable cookies so that service companies can access personal data and register digital copies of their purchases. With this legalized framework it is a lot harder to freely scrub private data from inboxes. Partly due to privacy breaches in the early days of the digital era, most people have developed a negative attitude towards data used without their consent, Ishwari Thopte says. People believe that the less data is accessible to companies the better. Understanding data profitability over a longer-term, and which solutions can be gained in exchange for access to data, is significant for innovation to emerge. Startups have tried numerous ways to overcome a block in data usage, asking customers to take a picture and upload the data by themselves or by visiting them at home to collect information. For a value-based consumption ecosystem to evolve, the scarcity of personal data needs a consistent process to collect and safely utilize it. Once customers adopt this ritual and upload the data on their own, digitalizing a wardrobe after every fashion purchase will become easier.

# LEASE CONCEPT

The rental subscription model for fashion can be beneficial for businesses and customers. The well-known dilemma of having a limited wardrobe and storage spaces in the UK encourages people to try the rental service to free up space and find pleasure in styling new urban outfits. The return of garments can be done under the current system, making additional savings on utilities for garment care. The service providers, in fact, take full responsibility for the care process. A new generation of startups is emerging on the UK market that see great potential in positioning fashion consumption on a rental subscription model which needs to gain popularity in order to be more affordable.

Nevertheless, before this service came in a standalone format, it was offered on independent online platforms with established service conditions of price, lease period, number of garments in the bundle, and regularity for change. The lease concept in fashion was born in the Netherlands in the territory of circular denim brand, MUD Jeans. This conscious brand was a pioneer in the denim world with provocative ideas on the consumption process, but it was also a management instrument for the collecting, sorting, and recycling or potential reuse of its produced denim. MUD Jeans denim is designed from

Photo: MUD Jeans

post-consumer waste, with 60 percent organic cotton fibre and 40 percent cotton from recycled jeans in the current fabric composition. This is only the beginning as it is a personal goal for Bert van Son, the brand's CEO, to complete the research and make denim with pure 100 percent post-consumer waste. Just look at the level of development achieved over time; when the brand started seven years ago, their denim fabric content contained only 20 percent recycled worn jeans. To stimulate the return of discarded garments produced by any brands, MUD Jeans employ an incentive system. Customers can return any brands' used jeans, as long as the fabric composition is known, and in return receive a 10 euro discount for a new pair of MUD Jeans. The jeans must be made of at least 96% of cotton, van Son says. In this way, customers can be certain their garments are recovered in the recycling loop. The denim collecting points are spread around its online store and retail network of 300 partners in 28 countries. The lease concept activation is ensured by an annual membership subscription, where service users pay only for the wear of the garment. In contrast to an ordinary sales model, where customers become the sole owner of purchased garments, the lease concept is turning ownership and responsibility over to the brand, encouraging customers to utilize the service instead. After a year, leased denim can be kept, returned or swapped for a new pair and repaired free of charge in Germany, Netherlands, Belgium throughout the duration of the leasing period.

Once jeans are returned, their condition is examined to define the appropriate cycle. Products in good condition are cleaned and sold in the brand's local vintage store, offering an opportunity to restyle vintage denim by applying patches. He points out that "the best way of recycling is to use the product for what [it] is made for and extend the lifecycle of the product [for] as long as possible". Garments unsuitable for reuse are shipped every month or two for recycling.

The impact of MUD Jeans' circular business model is estimated based on their annual sales turnover and circulation of jeans. "We sell around 50,000 pairs and more than 3,000 leased jeans", van Son explains. While the annual production of the denim market numbers 2 billion pairs of jeans, at first glance MUD Jeans is almost invisible. Considering the media coverage, news has been intelligently spreading the information in order to give a good example of a functional business model, in the hope that other brands reconsider their own performance. MUD Jeans has become an inspiring example on everyone's lips when it comes to a sustainability to follow.

Photo: MUD Jeans

# 3. SUSTAINABLE DESIGN AND STYLE

To operate effectively in sustainable design on a local level, creative influencers have to be well connected with social, environmental, material and economic forces. In reality, fashion creators collaborate with several countries while they develop new designs. Some brands are inspired by Indian textile traditions and prints, others are celebrating Indonesian artisan crafts or Peruvian handmade skills. Any choice made, like sourcing craft and materials overseas, enhances a specific region's economics and keeps artisanal work alive. When it comes to local material resources, it's rare that a designer can get access to all the desired and exclusive fabrics, unless they are citizens of a competitive textile hub country or a major capital. Consequently, not all influencers from smaller markets or businesses speak the same language as the industrial textile world, sometimes they prefer to avoid it and place fabric orders with small family workshops or create them themselves.

In a local economic and ecological context, companies are testing different upcycling and recycling initiatives to address a situation of overstock inventory arising from tons of post-consumer waste and to tackle pre-consumer production waste. Historically, apparel textiles have been difficult to recycle due to the uncertain origins of the fabric content. Most fabrics are blended with synthetic and natural fibres, like cotton with rayon or polyester with cotton. To process mixed fibres into new products, they should be separated, explains Heather Kaye, founder of LOOP swim. The brand creates knitted swimwear fabrics made of 87% recycled PET and 13% Spandex, which are not only recycled but also recyclable. Spandex is burnt by enzymes and the pure content is used for other purposes, like insulation, or in the production of carpets and upholstery, Kaye says. In Asia, the brand plans to collect swimwear which has reached the end of its life, in collaboration with retail partners with instore collection points. The products will join the local recycling stream in Hong Kong, while in the USA market products will be recycled by LOOP swim yarn producer, Unifi. Another UK based company, kidswear brand Bundlee, is exploring the deconstruction and reconstruction of garments that can't be used in their current state anymore. The Bundlee subscription model allows customers to return the product. In this way, the brand takes ownership of the whole lifecycle, from managing the production of kidswear with sustainably made fabrics to upcycling it.

In the footwear sector, the situation is more complex. In the early 90s, the footwear industry had the first fully compostable shoes created by German shoemaker family, Thies. With 163 years of experience in the field, the company constantly evolved and was able to improve its footwear offer. Recycling footwear also means reusing byproduct waste generated in other industries. Instead of burning or throwing away fish skins, for instance, they are veggie tanned to become the strongest leather in Thies footwear. Also, unused milk is recycled into milk fibre that has a better functionality than regular felt, Sebastian Thies says. Alternatives to leather can be upcycled cannabis or grass, which grows extensively in hayfields. Used coffee grounds too can be recycled to become animal-free leather. Thies explains, "coffee itself is not a harmful product. [You just need to be sure] where the coffee is coming from and how people are treated". Perhaps a shocking approach to show society what can be done with waste is oxblood, in French "sang de bœuf". In ancient times pigments were a common material for printing, and painting the exterior of farmhouses in Scandinavia, or the indoor floors of old Berlin houses that were covered in brown and red colours, with oxblood as protection for wood, he says. Today, animal blood can be found in abundance due to the meat industry, but it is thrown away without ever being used. "There is no respect for nature or for the animals" Thies says, stressing the importance of not wasting such a product. The experimental shoe made with oxblood bio leather is not for sale, but is a pure and direct message to the industry and society about the wealth of natural materials that could be used. "There is no difference, if you consume milk, meat or leather, you can also consume blood". All the parts should be used rationally, either you use them all or none of them, he adds. According to this credo, Thies' nat-2 footwear brand produces footwear for the vegan audience and those looking for ecologically made products. From a footwear perspective, vegan doesn't mean ecological, they are two different strands, but people often confuse the two, Thies says. Vegan sympathies in fashion are usually directed only towards animals, not towards the sustainability aspects. Think of what role sustainability plays for animals. It's the same whether you eat a monkey or kill the tree where the monkey lives; the monkey is going to die anyway without the tree, Thies explains.

Footwear recycling, or compostability as it is known according to Cradle to Cradle principles, is not feasible at the moment due to the lack of centralized infrastructure for end customers to return it. People are purchasing sustainable products, but they don't return them to the appropriate collection points for recycling, because they hardly exist. In the end, these products end up in flea markets, if they are not thrown away like any other shoe. The transfer of knowledge about product values, if its Cradle to Cradle or recyclable, is lost for the next buyer. Also, compostable footwear materials can take up to 80-100 years to decompose, Thies says, opening another discussion about whether this really makes sense and whether anybody would do it. Post-consumer footwear could never be recycled 100 percent, but it can achieve 80 percent, Thies adds. For example, in Germany, he continues, a specialized recycling company is able to deconstruct any typology of shoe - traditionally made, compostable, Cradle to Cradle or recyclable shoes - into separate elements, like metal, outsoles, insoles, thanks to a machine which sorts them and puts them in separate piles. From a production perspective, it is really important to use materials that are already made from recycled materials, he concludes, so to ease the process and reduce the usage of virgin materials.

Footwear designer Marita Setas Ferro admits flexibility in the material choice is essential. During material selection for shoe soles, she evaluates the quality of materials and already thinks about the best way to reuse them. For instance, natural rubber is a biological material with comfortable and soft characteristics, and it can be recycled together with other materials, although for other types of products only. She uses cork in shoe platforms and remnants of production are recycled into wall covers for exteriors. This is how the footwear industry can feed other industries and support them, in a closed-loop system. Another consideration is to what extent certain materials are in line with customer demands. Recycled soles with PU are produced in a single black

Photo: nat-2™

colour, although the market wants to have the same colour for the shoe upper and the sole. Setas Ferro, for instance, designs winter collections with this option. This is a way in which sustainable design can address the primary cause of the waste issue with overhead planning and a forecasting process, so as to be aligned with end users' demands. This principle is adopted in various design approaches. The nat-2 footwear brand has invented the world's first two-in-one shoe, giving freedom to customers to expand wearability through day-to-day scenarios. The upper and outsole of the shoes are in fact removable and can be easily switched to give a casual, sporty, or travel look. In addition, customers don't need to buy a new pair of shoes. Understanding customer preferences in the first place helps brands to produce truly desirable products, while co-creation is becoming a democratic way to meet the precise expectations of customers. Away To Mars is an independent co-creation platform inviting both designers and customers to join the creation process. Anyone is allowed to bring their creative ideas to the table and contribute to the making of the desired final product. From all inputs, Away To Mars generates a selection process to define the outstanding creative expressions to market with the new items. Successful candidates earn a percentage from produced and sold out collections. This is a win-win situ-

Photo: nat-2™

ation, where customers are empowered with the possibility to express their own imagination in the design process, while brands get to better understand their customers, and only produce what is needed. A fashion world with so many options doesn't need a traditional design approach anymore, says Thies, but rather a new generation of products needs to have sustainability in its DNA. If businesses want to exist in the future, they have to innovate, to catalyze change – without progression, the product offer will remain the same, at the same retail locations. What really has changed today is our perception and interest towards innovative products which are broadly being covered in the press. Most of these developments existed for 30 years, but nobody was interested in spending money and effort on them, he continues.

## SUSTAINABLE STYLE

These designs, coming from diverse locations and a variety of cultures, showcase a reality of sustainable fashion that appeals to customers' needs and it's evolving from a niche to a wider market segment. As already mentioned, according to geographical origin, whether it's India, UK, Germany, Slovenia, The Netherlands, Czech Republic, Shanghai, Cambodia, Singapore, Ireland, Sweden, the creative influencers shape conscious lifestyles in different ways, respecting the unique elements of their own culture, needs, regional style, and authentic, individual desires. The diversity of individual designers is a strength for the fashion ecosystem, a system where anyone can express creativity freely. For a style to last for future generations, designers are evaluating the whole picture to balance the laws of simplicity, comfort in appeal, and feeling, and also trans-seasonal relevance to offer the possibility of wearing the same garment in multiple ways; like how a pair of shoes can suit both casual and business attire, or a trans-seasonal pair of jeans. A thoughtful, valuable attempt to design for multiplicity, instead of fitting one type of aesthetic, is providing more style possibilities and more visual expressions. This is especially true when living in such a diverse environment, speaking different languages, working in all types of industries and having different points of view. We used to be inspired by other cultures, forms of art, or exciting experiences when introducing uncommon elements into our lifestyle. A similar approach is required for sustainable design, to integrate a broad perspective in a mass customized product. Just think of one typology of a successful commercial style offered by all designers and brands. What distinctive aesthetic will this style have? If a fashion buyer looks at a product from a well-known, successful brand, they can easily distinguish its unique aesthetic, created to satisfy the needs of customers, that the brand is known for. If other brands only replicated the successful aesthetic of a certain brand, without distinguishing themselves, the fashion world would have a lot of clones and tedious monotony.

# KNITWEAR

**Graciela Huam** knitwear goes well with any denim, silk, or linen outfit. Elegant and sophisticated, this street style is a mix of Dutch and Peruvian traditions. It experiments with traditional Peruvian craftsmanship by merging handmade knitwear techniques and local raw resources: Alpaca, baby Alpaca, and the sought-after Pima Cotton. All these traditional elements are then combined with exclusive design patterns to suit European tastes. To predict potential demand for Alpaca style, the designer keeps an eye on recent trends that are enhancing the value of classic knitwear ranges to meet the desires of present and future generations.

**Cardigan & Sweater:** Graciela Huam | **Ingredients:** 100% alpaca
**Palazzo Pants:** Graciela Huam | **Ingredients:** 98% cotton drill and 2% polyester
**Earring:** WISP | **Ingredients:** sterling silver Glass orbs hold sensual perfume

# SWIMWEAR

To make an impact on the entire product category, **LOOP swim** uses a single yarn in a signature woven and knitted PET fabric. Recycled PET is a modern version of virgin polyester, consisting of post-consumer plastic bottles collected after use and transformed into new yarns. This way, swimwear becomes part of the solution because it uses recycled polyester with the same technical performance as virgin polyester fibres. Longevity of fabric, colour fastness and a soft feel is the brand's signature mix.

**Bikini:** Loop swim | **Ingredients:** 87% REPREVE® recycled PET and 13% creroa® highclo™ spandex

# SENSUAL TECH

**WISP** wearable sensual jewellery produces a multi-sensory experience, enhancing the journey of desire for female sexual liberation; SENS sterling silver jewellery worn on the ear, neck or finger stimulate specific pressure points and erogenous zones to achieve the desired mood: to feel energized, trigger arousal or relieve tension. The future of intimacy is only limited by our imagination and desired lifestyle. Most of the jewellery components are made from recyclable materials and refillable organic ingredients, such as avocado or coconut oil in reusable perfume orbs.

**Overall:** La feme MiMi  |  **Ingredients:** 100% wool
**Necklace:** WISP  |  **Ingredients:** sterling silver *Stone*: violet amethyst

# FOOTWEAR

Style and comfort cushion formula in a **Funky Kalakar** shoe reflects the continuity expected from a pair of shoes to be worn on multiple occasions. The brand is sourcing only vegan, natural materials and waste resources under the auspices of PETA. Jute mixed with cotton, canvas or organic cotton is used for the upper shoe, while they fill the lining and outer portions with natural fabrics to achieve a high breathability factor. The mountain of car tyres regu-

**Long Shirt Dress:** Kozii  |  **Ingredients:** 100% organic cotton with block print
**Ankle Strap Shoe:** Funky Kalakar  |  **Ingredients:** *Upper material*: handloom cotton *Lining*: cotton fabric *Insole*: upcycled soft cushion padding *Sole*: upcycled rubber from scrap tyres

**Flat Shoes:** Marita Moreno | **Ingredients:** *Upper material*: bio-leather *Lining:* bio-leather *Insole:* PU sponge *Sole:* rubber | **T-Shirt Sweater:** Elsien Gringhuis | **Ingredients:** 100% organic cotton cuff and triangle: 95% organic cotton and 5% elastan | **Short:** Elsien Gringhuis | **Ingredients:** 55% hemp and 45% organic cotton

larly replaced once every two years inspired the brand's environmental effort to reduce landfill pollution and improve the performance of shoes. Properly cleaned car tyres are upcycled into slip-free, highly durable shoe soles.

Sustainability, comfort, and design are three elements **Marita Moreno** carefully adopts in footwear production. Taking customers on a tour into Portuguese culture, heritage and selected local quality materials make for the best experience in shoes. Bio leather, cork, and microfibre are the preferred raw materials for a vegan lifestyle. The innovative potential of rich Portuguese design lies in the combination of technological and ancient regional handicraft techniques from the Azores, Minho, Alentejo, and results in a fine expression of luxury.

**Luxury Sneakers:** nat-2™ | **Ingredients:** *Upper material*: Delphinium leaves/Rittersporn Petals, Hayfield, glass and man-made, recycled PET bottles *Lining*: Bio-Ceramic® *Insole*: real cork *Sole*: rubber
**White Reflective:** nat-2™ | **Ingredients:** *Upper material*: finest Nappa leather *Lining & insole*: smooth leather & real cork *Outsole*: 100% real rubber
**V-Neck Dress & Trousers:** Elsien Gringhuis | **Ingredients:** 55% hemp 45% organic cotton | **Graphical Striped Shirt & Skirt:** Elsien Gringhuis | **Ingredients:** 100% organic cotton

**nat-2** is an avant-garde, high-end fashionable footwear brand experimenting with unique novelty materials, that nobody has really ever used for shoes before: wood, glass, olive leather, moss etc. Seasonless, genderless sneaker styles are fairly produced and handmade in Italy, with the factories sourcing all the key materials from the surrounding area. Special by-products from fruit, flowers or coffee come from Austria, other materials from Germany. Its sustainable design is defined in just three sneaker silhouettes and a single fit for the perfect shoe. Unchanged styles are upgraded only with new materials and colours, and sold with no fitting issue for anyone.

# STREETWEAR

**Plant Faced Clothing** beliefs are subtly spread in unique, on-trend T-shirts and hoodies with timeless streetwear prints, using water-based and vegan-friendly inks on ethically sourced textiles or Fair Wear certified organic cotton. For Plant Faced Clothing, working with streetwear implies being in constant motion, as fast as streetwear trends. The latest news in style and frequent travel help the designer to feel the speed of street style change in diverse locations and cultures.

**Scarves:** Cocccon | **Ingredients:** 100% peace silk with block print
**Leather Jackets:** Olivenleder | **Ingredients:** chrome-free lamb leather tanned with olive extract
**Knitted Dress:** Benedetti Life | **Ingredients:** 100% organic cotton
**Palazzo Pants:** Graciela Huam | **Ingredients:** 98% cotton drill, 2% polyester

**Look (left)**
**Dungarees:** Lucy & Yak  |  **Ingredients:** 60% organic cotton, 40% viscose
**T-shirt:** PLANT FACED  |  **Ingredients:** 100% organic cotton
**Sneakers:** GRAND STEP SHOES  |  **Ingredients:** *Upper material*: vegetable tanned leather *Lining & insock*: chrome-free leather *Outsole*: 100% rubber
**Bracelet:** PURNAMA  |  **Ingredients:** 98% recycled inner tube *Buttons*: strong metal fastening and non-corrosive buttons

**Look (right)**
**High Waisted Twill Jeans:** Lucy & Yak  |  **Ingredients:** 100% organic cotton
**Classic Tee:** Filippa K  |  **Ingredients:** 100% cotton
**White Reflective Sneakers:** nat-2™  |  **Ingredients:** *Upper material*: finest Nappa leather *Lining & insole*: smooth leather & real cork *Outsole*: 100% real rubber

# CRAFTSMANSHIP

To ensure the design is timeless and original, **Good Krama** starts by sourcing Cambodian materials, like handmade fabrics, traditionally woven on looms, or selected remnants, and the deadstock of fabrics stored in local garment factories. The traditional craftsmanship aspect is also nurtured by the brand which has a strong connection with the environment of the Takeo Province of Cambodia, where the textiles are woven. The woven component is always part of a garment which can be added either as a small detail or it can constitute the entire garment. This work is fundamental in developing apprenticeships to help restore these lost craft skills among local communities that want to be financially independent.

**Tunic:** Mateja Benedetti | **Ingredients:** 100% organic cotton with a water-based floral print
**Trousers:** Mateja Benedetti | **Ingredients:** 100% organic cotton
**Wedge Sandals:** Marita Moreno | **Ingredients:** *Upper material*: Leather and textured leather *Sole*: Rubber *Insole*: Leather *Lining*: Leather *Platform*: Cork

**Skirt:** IMRECZEOVA  |  **Ingredients:** 100% silk
**Bodysuit:** GOOD KRAMA  |  **Ingredients:** 100% upcycled cotton elastane fabric
**Jacket:** GOOD KRAMA  |  **Ingredients:** 100% upcycled brocade fabric - exact fibre unknown *Lining*: 100% upcycled cotton
**Flat Shoes:** Marita Moreno  |  **Ingredients:** *Upper material*: bioleather *Lining*: bioleather *Insole:* PU sponge *Sole*: rubber

# BLOCK PRINT

To give mulberry silk its uniqueness, **The Ethical Silk Company** uses block print for handcrafted luxury, embracing handmade pieces with imperfections and differences. Nightwear styles are easily transformed into casual garments to wear during the day. Palazzo pants can obtain a glamorous look when paired with strappy sandals and a silk top, or a silk shirt with a pair of jeans. Silk garments can even be styled for both weddings or an evening out.

**Pyjamas, Loungewear Set:** The Ethical Silk Company | **Ingredients:** 100% mulberry silk with block print, natural (undyed) colour
**Mule:** Funky Kalakar | **Ingredients:** *Upper material*: jute cotton *Lining*: cotton fabric *Insole*: upcycled soft cushion padding
**Ankle Strap Shoe:** Funky Kalakar | **Ingredients:** *Upper material*: handloom cotton *Lining*: cotton fabric *Insole*: upcycled soft cushion padding *Sole*: upcycled rubber from scrap tyres

**Kozzi's** mindful signature concept holds onto a free style idea which comes in one size that fits different body types. As a matter of personal style preferences, items can be worn on a particular occasion or chic event. Kozzi loves to experiment with colours in vegetable dyes and unique prints using ancient woodblock printing techniques. The next occasion to experiment in colour options for a more precise handmade feel in print will be serigraphy, as an alternative to block print.

**Maxi Dress:** Kozii  |  **Ingredients:** 100% modal with block print

# MADE TO ORDER

Easy to combine and adapt to any styles without losing the brand signature, **Elsien Gringhuis** creates ageless styles using the made to order principle. Personal design is what the clients appreciate the most. They are ready to wait 5 to 10 working days before getting their hands on self-defined style. Its collections blurs the line between timeless and ageless so as to be suitable for people from their 20s to their 80s. On the business side, the advantages of the made to order principle is minimizing unwanted stock and the risks of sales discounts.

**Scarf**: Cocccon   |   **Design:** Hemma Seifried and Georg Andreas Suhr
**Ingredients:** 100% peace satin silk
**Anorak:** Elsien Gringhuis   |   **Ingredients:** 100% wool *Ribbing*: 90 % cotton, 10% elastane
**Tube Skirt:** Elsien Gringhuis   |   **Ingredients:** 100% wool
**Boots:** Marita Moreno   |   **Ingredients:** leather and pleated leather *Lining & insole*: leather *Outsole:* textured leather

**Boilersuit:** Lucy & Yak | **Ingredients:** 100% organic cotton
**Sneakers:** Marita Moreno | **Ingredients:** *Upper material*: white varnishing microfibre and white hexagon microfibre *Sole*: rubber *Insole*: PU Sponge *Lining*: anti-transpiration microfibre

**Coat:** IMRECZEOVA | **Ingredients:** 70% wool, 10% cashmere, 20% PAD
**Waterproof Rain Boots:** Nat-2™ | **Ingredients:** *Upper material*: mix of rubber and recycled leather *Lining & insole*: synthetic textile *Outsole*: rubber

**Polo Dress:** Mateja Benedetti   |   **Ingredients:** 100% organic cotton with water-based digital printing
**Flat Shoes:** Marita Moreno   |   **Ingredients:** *Upper material*: bio-leather microfibre and white hexagon microfibre *Lining*: Bio-leather *Insole*: PU Sponge *Sole*: Rubber

# UPCYCLING

**Purnama** Indonesian batik artworks are handcrafted by women in Nepal. Upcycled tyres or inner tubes are used to make pretty bracelets that are waterproof accessories suitable for sports activities, urban wear, or travel, with no prescribed seasonality. A sustainable environmental design aims to reduce the harmful effects of waste in Singapore in a simple way, by using alternatives to animal-based products that certified by PETA and supported by a company repair service.

**Kimono-Style Jacket & Dress:** Kozii | **Ingredients:** 100% organic cotton with block print
**Waterproof Rain Boots:** nat-2™ | **Ingredients:** *Upper material*: mix of rubber & recycled cork *Lining*: real cork *Insole*: synthetic textile *Outsole*: rubber
**Unisex Pants & Bodysuit:** GOOD KRAMA | **Ingredients:** 100% viscose, handwoven cotton krama pockets, 100% upcycled cotton elastane fabric
**Top & Pants:** Graciela Huam | **Ingredients:** 30% alpaca, 70% Tanguis cotton, 100% Pima cotton
**Sandals:** GRAND STEP SHOES | **Ingredients:** *Upper material, Lining & insole*: vegetable tanned leather *Outsole*: ethylene vinyl acetate

**Kaftan:** Kozii | **Ingredients:** 100% modal with block print
**Trousers:** Kozii | **Ingredients:** 100% organic cotton with block print
**Wedge Sandals:** Marita Moreno | **Ingredients:** *Upper material*: leather and textured leather *Sole*: rubber *Insole*: leather *Lining*: leather *Platform*: cork
**Bracelet:** PURNAMA | **Ingredients:** 98% recycled inner tube *Buttons*: strong metal fastenings and noncorrosive buttons

# THE ROLE OF COLOUR IN FASHION DESIGN

To be an active player in sustainable design, one should be fully aware of the set of mechanisms that govern the fashion system. Understanding what to improve and how to make a difference become the prerogative when attempting to shake well-established realities. Sandy MacLennan, a colour forecast consultant, has been active in the colour field for 30 years. In this book, he explains the role colour plays in fashion design, its coexistence with responsible ideas and its impact on seasonality and customer purchases.

## THE 24-MONTH CYCLE

The creative process of colour forecasting starts 24 months ahead of the retail season. It's an industry practice written in stone, repeating its cycle twice a year – for summer and winter collections. Progressing from a source of inspiration to a final product, colour forecasting is utilised in all stages of creation, from fabric production to garment design and range development. This is because colour, in its purest form, has the power to create meaning - it can give a garment an entirely new feel or appeal. In Europe, on a local level, independent consultants and designers involved in day-to-day business with brands in the retail and media fields form the concepts for the colour theme of the approaching season. The British Textile Colour Group, for instance, is a place where these ideas are sparked and shared to form a consensus on colour development, says MacLennan, a founding member of the organization. MacLennan identifies the creative process as a personal experience which starts with a blank page, followed by a set of questions: "What's new for me? What do I enjoy? What do I think is new about something?" From there, the local decision on colour goes to Intercolor, where a single country is ready to share a freewheeling idea representing that country at that moment with an international audience. By trying to tell the story of a particular city at a particular moment, or conveying a sort of cultural zeitgeist, colour consultants express an imagined future through different shades.

Those extremely important topics that appear in the news, like schoolchildren who strike for climate change, influence future colour trends. After viewing video clips, Intercolor's international members make a collective decision on which iconic visions to develop. Individual consultants pass these ideas down the fashion chain – new colours acquire new meaning in skilled industry hands and gain significance among the customer base. Even the colour themes that considerably mutate in terms of shade still retain a flavour of the initial idea, MacLennan says. Within 18 to 20 months, yarn and fibre manufacturers appear on the colour chain. These players need to update themselves all the time to stay ahead of seasons, MacLennan explains. To formulate a theme for a new collection, manufacturers, together with colour forecasters, begin a journey painted with the broad brushstrokes of provocative elements. Looking into families of colours – like warm khakis, warm greys, cold ice, whites, navies and blacks – these basic colours are modified by one or two elements to create a little excitement for the coming season. In the end, only a few strong elements will survive and shape the final colour palette that will eventually reach stores and end customers.

Spinning, weaving and knitting companies are next in the chain to work with colour. After an 18-month cycle, the final fabrics are showcased at the most important trade shows, like Milano Unica, Munich Fabric Start and Première Vision, where designers make their fabric selection and bring back samples. Within the next three months, new collections are ready to be presented at fashion shows.

## COLOUR AND SUSTAINABILITY

Sustainability joins the colour cycle only at a later stage. Giving colour forecasters space to form their proposals during the exploratory phase allows them to find that nugget of inspiration that will drive and animate them through the realization stage. MacLennan discloses that there are certain colour categories the textile industry has to keep off the agenda. Local legislation already forbids the use of the heavy metals and fluorescent chemicals required to achieve bold colours. On the other hand, science and technology must become strong allies to really push the boundaries of sustainable fashion. The fields of bacteriology and bioscience, for example, can teach us a lot, especially when it comes to colour. Even studying how insects and plants create pigments in nature can give valuable insight on how to create new shades in a more responsible way.

## INTEGRATING COLOUR INTO TEXTILE COLLECTIONS

Colour is a tool in the textile field, and this tool generates profit. Since all collections are sold on the basis of colour, textile producers have established a system of almost predetermined sales. They simply divide a single collection into two categories: commercial textiles and seasonal textiles. Commercial textiles only get a slight adjustment in colour on a seasonal basis, meaning that classic colours like "navy might get rethought and made a little bit cooler. Red might become cool and a bit greener", MacLennan explains. The other category reflects the innovation, risk and excitement implemented by colour forecasters, although, maybe only "one or two colours are incredibly successful", he continues. MacLennan believes in the importance of basic shades, but thinks new colours are equally important, as they are a vital ingredient for beginning the innovation process, even for a well-established brand. If manufacturers kept only the classic range in search for profit, their brands wouldn't have their unique creative voice.

## DESIGNERS AND FINAL CUSTOMERS

As MacLennan says, even consumer shopping behaviours are often based on colour, as it creates a natural appeal to the eye. When people like what they see, "they feel a little bit more loyal towards the brand", he says. As a rule, a basis of classics that underpin the brand makes up the bestseller category, along with darker monochrome and denim colours, and either black or navy. Another two or three luscious tints are identified as the particular

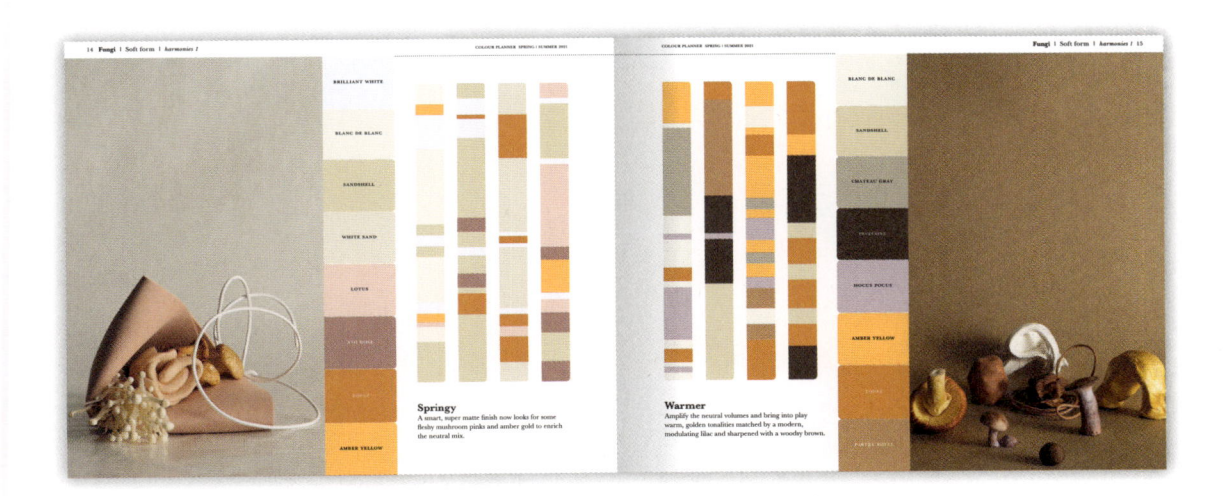

Photo: Aaron Tilley / aarontilley.com

signature of a brand, and those shades are adjusted a little each season to create new nuances in the colour offering. This approach assures a colour palette that reflects consumer desires – it ensures customers don't feel alienated, but perceive the new products as a fashion pitch. MacLennan finds that consumer shopping habits are repetitive in nature: we tend to forget what we purchased the previous year and shop for "things that we bought before without realizing it".

Signature colours have another objective: that of reaching the press. Eye-catching, candy colours are often selected for editorials and TV promotion. MacLennan highlights that "all these colours have to be selected through research and trials before they end up in stores" and only the brands that learn the rules and play the colour game in a dynamic way have commercial success, he adds. Gucci, for instance, proves that its approach to experimenting with colours not only pays well in terms of public success and selling rates, but also that there is no crime in having more colours, if done in a responsible way.

## **NATURAL COLOURS**

Fashion is an industry where all begins with colour in some way. It's imperative for people working on sustainable design to acquire a sensitive approach towards colour and have access to healthier dyes. To underpin the principle of sustainability for colours and materials, MacLennan has developed a section rooted in the story of fungi for PANTONE VIEW COLOUR PLANNER see page 73 - the trendbook for colour forecasting. MacLennan's contribution is an entire aesthetic inspired by blooming summer mushrooms, infusing a contemporary appeal with timeless value, featuring soft neutrals and plant-based colours ranging from calm white to beige and taupe tones. These colour stories weren't tested, but MacLennan knows they can be easily achieved by using plant-based dyes.

# 4. FABRICS AND MATERIALS

This chapter covers the values of fashion fabrics, the way they are sourced, used as pure ingredients or blended with other fibres. It's an in-depth review of the most used textiles in fashion design, as well as some of the most innovative alternative solutions recently introduced by industry experts and innovators.

Prepare to get a taste of the industry perspective and appreciate each step of the process, from the sourcing of raw materials and the production journey of textiles, to the authentic values and peculiarities of fabrics. Most importantly, discover how innovative manufacturing processes are reducing environmental impact, as designers have the power to reduce waste and increase product sustainability by understanding and choosing the right textiles.

As of today, the available public data assessing the environmental impact of each fabric does not consider the care for the garment, nor other factors that could have an impact on the final usage and disposal. This work is still in progress, as industries, textile associations and manufacturers are in search of definitive life cycle assessment results.

To completely understand a garment's content, and for a chance to prolong the longevity of future products, some industry players give a little incentive under the form of general care advice.

# GLOBAL FIBRE CONSUMPTION

**1.1%**
WOOL

**4.8%**
OTHER NATURAL FIBRES

**6.3%**
WOOD-BASED CELLULOSIC FIBRES

**25.3%**
COTTON

**62.5%**
SYNTHETIC FIBRES

SOURCES: ICAC, CIRFS, TFY, FEB.

# COTTON

Soft. Breathable. Comfortable. Absorbent. Versatile. Organic. These are just a few of the adjectives used to describe cotton, the textile industry's second most popular fibre. In 2017, the world produced more than 25 million tonnes of cotton that were used to make just about anything – from dollar bills, cotton swabs, and coffee filters to T-shirts, lingerie, and denim.

Cotton has been hailed as the paragon of natural fibres, as its production does not require extensive chemical processes and it's organically biodegradable. But in recent years, this paragon has received flak from environmental organizations that pointed out that the world's over-reliance on this fluffy white crop has led to high amounts of water and energy waste, water pollution, pesticide and chemical runoff contamination, and controversial labour conditions.

Archaeologists found the first evidence of cotton use in a Pakistani Neolithic funeral chamber that dates to around 5500 B.C. From that moment, the fibre gradually permeated human societies as each year brought new developments to the slow, arduous task of separating the fibres from the seeds. In the 16th century, the invention of the worm-gear roller cotton gin, a machine that is still widely used today to separate seeds from fibres, jump-started the cotton fever when it was introduced in India. From then on, the industry grew exponentially, skyrocketing in the 1760s, when new ways to efficiently spin yarns were invented. "The Industrial Revolution came with [...] cotton, and then as you know, capitalism was built out of the Industrial Revolution – and the most billable material in the world was [...] cotton", explains Santi Mallorquí, CEO of Organic Cotton Colours (OCC). In 1793, cotton's transformation into an incredibly profitable venture that world pow-

Photo: Monstera Estudi: Ángel Martínez Moreno

ers would capitalize on immediately was complete. The American South, in particular, took advantage of this opportunity, ushering over 1.8 million slaves into cotton fields who were used to harvest and manufacture large quantities of the magic fibre.

Today's cotton production has come a long way since the 19th century. Innovations like the mechanical harvesting machine, new dyeing and finishing procedures, pesticides, labour regulations and genetically modified seeds have altered the industry, for better or for worse. Conventional cotton production is responsible for 10 percent of the planet's pollution, according to Organic Cotton Colour's website. In response to these changes in conventional production, key industry actors have begun to push for better cotton.

## CONVENTIONAL VS . ORGANIC COTTON: WHAT'S THE DIFFERENCE?

Conventional cotton is exactly what it sounds like — a fibre that is produced on a mass scale by conventional means. Because it needs to be produced on such a large, bulk and cheap scale, this type of cotton is associated with serious environmental problems. The first concern is that cotton is a thirsty crop that needs to be irrigated constantly. Studies have shown that it can take more than 2,700 litres of water to produce enough cotton for one T-shirt — water used not just for irrigation, but for pesticide application, processing and dyeing. Experts estimate that 60 percent of the world's cotton is grown in irrigated fields. High water consumption levels also mean high wastewater production which, if not treated correctly, can contaminate local freshwater supplies and negatively affect ecosystems and drinking water.

Contamination mostly comes from the high amounts of pesticides and fertilizers used in cotton fields. The cotton industry is responsible for 10 percent of the world's agricultural chemical usage. Most of these chemicals are toxic, and others are carcinogenic. The effects of these chemicals, combined with those used in the finishing process, have a much further reach than just the local communities they contaminate. They can remain in the fabric and affect end consumers, causing or aggravating skin problems like itching, eczema and rashes.

Although slavery has been officially abolished throughout the world, the conventional cotton industry is still plagued with labour code violations, especially in developing regions. In 2016, the U.S. Department of Labor reported that child or forced labour was used in 18 countries, including major producers like China, India, Pakistan and Brazil. Smaller farmers struggle to compete with fluctuating market prices and accumulate debt, especially since the introduction of expensive genetically modified (GMO) cotton seeds.

GMO cotton contains toxins that repel various pests, meaning farmers can supposedly spend less on pesticides. However, these seeds do not reproduce and new ones need to be bought every year. In most cases, additional pesticides, which can be more toxic than traditional ones, are still needed. In India, GMO cotton, which accounts for 89 percent of the country's crop growth, has been linked with the tragically high suicide rates among impoverished farmers. Over a quarter of a million Indian farmers have committed suicide since GMO cotton seeds were introduced 16 years ago, and experts are beginning to link the crushing debt generated by GMO farming with the mental health crisis.

> *"Organic cotton is a perfect way to bridge the gap between demand and sustainability by complying with stringent organic agricultural standards and certifications".*

Despite all of these problems, cotton is still the queen of fibres. Few synthetic fibres come close to its comfort, price and popularity. "The industry only produces what it really believes is going to be sold and [...] what is more well-known and [what] everyone is producing", Mallorquí says. Organic cotton is a perfect way to bridge the gap between demand and sustainability by complying with stringent organic agricultural standards and certifications. Most organic fibres must obtain Global Organic Textile Standard (GOTS) certifications. According to Textile Exchange's aboutorganiccotton.org initiative: "Its production sustains [soil] health, ecosystems and people by using natural processes rather than artificial inputs. Organic farming does not allow [for] the use of toxic chemicals or GMOs (genetically modified organisms)". A 2014 Life Cycle Assessment found that organic cotton helped reduce 46 percent of the contaminants contributing to global warming, 70 percent of field emissions from fertilizers, 91 percent of water consumption and 62 percent of energy consumption. Farmers have also reported better social outcomes when growing organic cotton.

# INNOVATION FROM THE PAST

A unique example of pure, organic cotton on the market right now is Organic Cotton Colours. When the company started 25 years ago, organic cotton was only in demand by people with sensitive skin problems, like dermatitis and eczema, which prevented them from using conventional options that might contain irritating toxins, Mallorquí recalls. Today, more and more consumers and retailers have begun demanding fabrics that, like OCC's cotton, are toxin-free and planet friendly. "All [of] these markets have been increasing and today, we are in a very powerful situation, in terms [of] everyone looking for these types of fabrics", he says.

## COLOUR GROUND COTTON

Over the years, OCC has become a one-stop shop for naturally coloured cotton. The brand offers yarn, fabric, manufacturing services and basic clothing items. All of their products are made from GMO-free cotton and sold in colours natural for cotton. Unlike most organic or conventional vendors, OCC does not bleach its products, but rather maintains cotton's off-white, ecru tint – its natural colour. "We have to keep offering pure fabrics – not treated, not processed – and which obviously perform as cotton performs. This is our innovation", Mallorquí says. Most consumers believe white is cotton's natural colour and view it as a symbol of purity. In reality, it's a product of the dyeing process, which is not respectful of the environment, he says. To keep their cotton pure, the brand does not use any type of dye, print or finish. Instead, they look to the future by preserving the past. Before chemical dyes were invented in the 19th century, cotton naturally grew in different colours like yellow, pink and black that people used to add flair to their creations. When it became obvious that dyeing was cheaper and

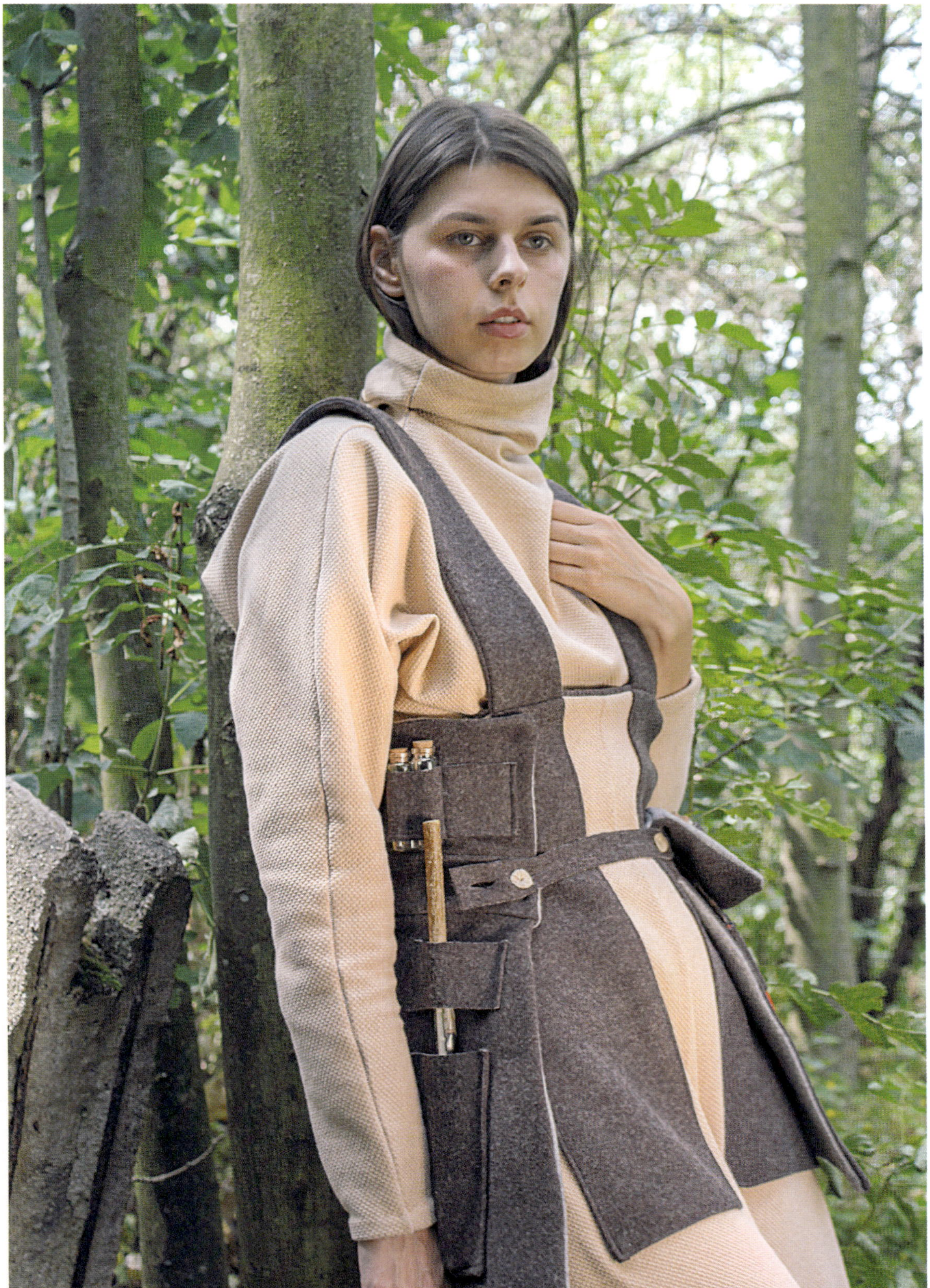

more profitable, governments and producers stopped cultivating coloured cotton and opted to grow traditional ecru cotton that could be easily dyed, losing many coloured varietals, Mallorquí explains. A few countries have tried to invest in recuperating natural, coloured cottons, like Peru, China, India and Brazil, with moderate success. Around 25 years ago, the Brazilian government invested in growing green and brown cotton – and OCC is committed to helping preserve this resource, the CEO proudly states. Without brands like OCC supporting preservation efforts, natural supplies would surely disappear over time. "We are very happy to also offer it as a solution to avoid[ing] the most harmful process in the textile industry, which is the dyeing process", he continues. The coloured cotton is blended with OCC's organic ecru cotton to make up for the coloured fibres' shorter dimensions. Most coloured ground cotton pieces are 75 percent coloured and 25 percent ecru, Mallorquí specifies. Coloured cotton is also unique in its sensitivity: since OCC does not apply any chemical finishes, the colour of the fabrics and garments is alive, and it intensifies with washes, wear and contact with light. The tonality of naturally coloured cotton will keep increasing for up to 20 washes. In contrast, chemically fixing colours makes them fade over time. While the shade of your product may change, the quality and durability of the yarn won't, he clarifies.

## THE BRAZILIAN PROJECT

Brazil's coloured cotton preservation initiative first caught OCC's attention, but the country's warm, hard-working farmers captured the company's heart. For the last 15 years, the company has been sourcing their raw materials almost exclusively from 200 families in the poor north-eastern region of the country. OCC has made a promise to each and every farmer: to buy all the cotton they produce, no matter what. This provides farmers with a stability that is rare in an industry where big brands frequently switch suppliers and buy organic cotton for the best price. OCC cultivates strong, long-lasting relationships with the farmers, many of whom share OCC's vision of growing cotton free of pesticides, as these chemicals damage the other crops they grow to support their livelihood. "We have a nice story to tell, because we know each farmer personally – we know who they are, we know their names, we know how they work", Mallorquí says. OCC has strict criteria that determines which farmers the brand is going to work with. For one, they need to own their own land. They also need to be growing other crops besides cotton to sustain their livelihoods, be registered with the Brazilian Ministry of Agriculture, obtain an Organic Brazil certification, and show that growing cotton is a way of life for them, not just a business, the CEO continues. These criteria were put in place to ward off the temptation to do business with large, industrial producers. Ultimately, there is a larger social benefit to working with many small farmers who will benefit from the extra income, he adds. OCC's objective is to keep increasing the number of families they support with the project – a goal that seems likely to be met if demand keeps growing. In 2018, OCC's sales swelled by 60 percent, while the conventional cotton market slowly decreased, Mallorquí says.

Because OCC oversees the cotton journey from seed to fibre to yarn to textile, they can offer full traceability with their products, especially since they have eliminated all the intermediaries often involved in the conventional production supply chain. Because OCC covers every step in the supply chain and provides its own material at each stage, individual designers and brands can source straight from the origin. This ensures the product has a full track record and no extra margin cost. In most cases, only bigger brands can buy farm fresh cotton, since it's a much more expensive source than the traditional open market. Mallorquí described how OCC had close relationships with different production units, which never failed to create high-quality cotton products lovingly grown in Brazil. "It's a new way of cultivating cotton", he explains. Working on the Brazil project, while rewarding, has not been easy, Mallorquí admits. Many of the farmers had never exported their cotton, so negotiating contracts with them was a long, complicated process, he reflects. At the beginning, establishing the right connection with every single farmer was also difficult, and it took around four years to build a direct relationship. Mallorquí and his team eventually overcame these challenges but were then faced with an even bigger one: getting GOTS certifications for 200 farmers was no piece of cake. Initially, the brand paid for each individual certification, but when overhead costs became too much, they decided to stop. Non-certified organic Brazilian cotton was already more expensive than GOTS certified cotton – Brazilian cotton shirts retail at around 30 Euros – so OCC introduced a new initiative: the OCC Guarantee Essential.

The OCC Guarantee is GOTS certified cotton sourced from Turkey, another supply that ensures the availability of GMO-free, organic yarns, "no matter the quantity of cotton we obtain from Brazil", Mallorquí explains, since annual harvests depend on weather conditions and other unpredictable aspects of agroecological cultivation. This option is perfect for brands that want to enter the market with organic, GOTS certified cotton but cannot wait for Brazilian fibres to be back in stock, or just want a slightly more affordable option. The lower prices are more profitable for the company and without these profits the Brazilian venture would not be financially sustainable. "Everything we do is to push the Brazilian project", he continues.

## WHAT THE FUTURE HOLDS

Trends show that the market will begin to turn to alternative solutions, like woven fabrics made from milk, aloe, banana, and corn, among other ingredients. However, one thing's clear to Mallorquí: cotton isn't going anywhere anytime soon. What will begin to change, in his opinion, are people's lifestyles. More and more people are starting to value physical wellbeing and look for toxin-free alternatives – which OCC most certainly is. "You can feel the difference when you are making the change to a culture of wellness consumption. This is something that is going to be trendy right now, and it's a really powerful direction that is going to change fast", he reflects. For the future, he hopes the brand will keep expanding, following the upward trends they've seen in recent years. Rather than focusing on larger clients, OCC is looking to work with small, upcoming businesses and individual designers, because the future of sustainable fashion is in the hands of "small brands, [and] small designers with a small production", he concludes.

## ▶ CARE ADVICE

Organic cotton is, above all else, normal cotton. Mallorquí recommends reducing the number of times you wash your clothes to make them last longer. He also suggests washing clothes at 30 degrees Celsius and avoiding chemical detergents and softeners.

# A COTTON SHIRT WITH A MODERN TWIST

It's like a scene from a romantic comedy: you're running late to an important meeting with your boss. It's a hot summer morning, and your train was late and packed to the brim. You're weaving your way through other commuters on the sidewalk when, suddenly, the worst happens – someone bumps into you and spills their coffee all over your pristine white cotton shirt. Flustered, annoyed, and sweating, you stumble into your boss's office, where your dishevelled attire raises some eyebrows.

This scenario could have gone a lot differently if you had just been wearing a shirt that was completely stain and sweat resistant. Fortunately, a French brand called INDUO has you covered with its innovative hydrophobic shirt fabric that repels stains and sweat marks. The fabric is the first of its kind that combines stain resistance with the breathability, softness, comfort, and biodegradability of cotton to create high-quality fabrics that are perfect for formal wear, dresses, and jackets.

Sustainability lies at INDUO's core — the idea sprang from a desire to reduce the production impact of a garment by extending its lifecycle as much as possible, explains brand founder Pauline Guesné. "The more wears we can get out of the garment, the more you diminish the environmental impact", she says. "This is what we're focused on, to create a fabric that is fresh and that you don't need to wash as often, because [...] bacteria won't develop in it like it does in a normal fabric".

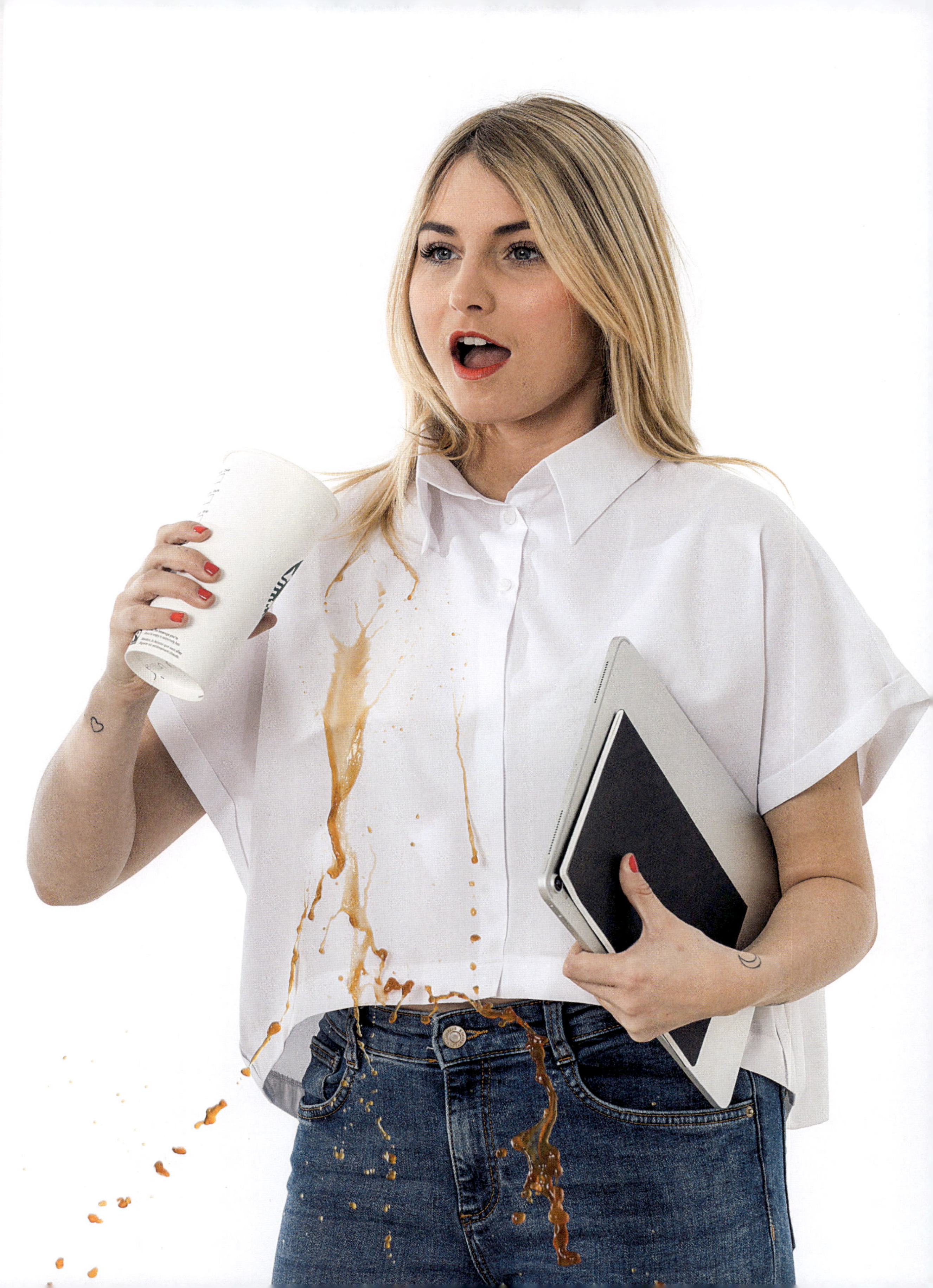

Guesné wanted to present a fresh, modern twist on traditional formalwear by incorporating technology and providing the market with better, sustainable alternatives. "You can do the same white plain shirt, but with a twist, […] like a traditional, timeless piece that you're going to wear for many years".

## PRODUCTION JOURNEY

INDUO fabrics start out the same way as other cotton textiles, as puffy white blossoms dotting the agricultural landscape. To date, they have exclusively sourced their raw material from China, since the country's humidity, heat, and water supply are perfect for producing the long, resistant fibres the impermeability process requires.

Once the high-end cotton arrives at the production plant, the fun begins. INDUO spins the yarn, and immediately begins treating it while adding dyes. All the dyeing must be done at the yarn level because once the chemicals are applied and the yarn becomes repellent, the colour no longer sticks, Guesné explains. There are so many treatments applied to the yarns to make cotton hydrophobic that INDUO can only work with two-ply yarns instead of single-ply ones. "The idea is really to use chemicals that are going to change the fibre but preserve its natural properties of softness and breathability", she continues. "We basically changed the shape of the cotton to do that". Most hydrophobic textiles have to be treated with toxic chemicals to enhance their properties, but INDUO's formula uses natural substances that do not damage the environment or the workers' health, Guesné says.

After these treatments, the yarn is woven into many different styles, including twill, herringbone, and Oxford. The product is then finished with treatments adapted from the military and medical sectors that solidify its hydrophobic properties, so it takes much longer to make than conventional fabrics, Guesné says. Because it takes so long, INDUO makes sure to stock several thousand metres of fabric in every colour they carry, which range from staple basics like white, blue, and pink to stripes and designs. Guesné lamented the fact that, because of the fibre's hydrophobic qualities, they cannot produce prints or patterns, slightly limiting design options for the time being.

## VALUE OF THE FABRIC

"Really the sweat resistance is [the] most impressive and amazing thing", Guesné says, when we asked about the fabric. "The fact that you're not wet, you don't feel wet, you feel fresh always and you don't have any stains showing – it's just the most amazing thing ever". By repelling sweat and other liquids, the fabric also prevents the development of bacteria that grow in humid environments and make normal clothes feel and smell dirty. It's this feature that lets you wear the shirt many times before washing it – in the Netherlands, customers have reported using their INDUO garments for up to two weeks without washing. The brand is so confident in their fabric's durability that they have a lifetime warranty customers can capitalize on if they find anything wrong with their product. In the three years that this innovative textile has been on the market, they have yet to hear any customer complaints in terms of the fabric's durability, she says proudly.

Another strength is that the fabric feels exactly like normal cotton, with the added benefit of liquid resistance. In blind tests, customers could not differentiate INDUO's fabric from normal cotton, and they were always surprised at its soft touch and feel, Guesné adds. Most of their clients tend to use the fabric for men's formal shirts, but some intrepid designers have gone further, creating dresses, jackets and full outfits out of the material. One designer has even begun to use gold yarn to embellish clothes, which preserves the fabric's properties and adds extra flair.

Currently, INDUO is targeting the market's premium sectors, both prêt-à-porter and tailor-made clothes. Their shirts can cost anywhere between €20 to €70 more than a traditional cotton dress shirt, Guesné estimates. For example, an IKKS essential cotton dress shirt costs €95, and an INDUO shirt costs €165 – a 74 percent price increase. Figaret Paris sells INDUO and an atelierprivé paris INDUO shirt costs 39 percent more than the regular line. She hopes that in the future they can produce more affordable options and expand to other garments, like trousers and suits, or incorporate new fibres like wool, alternative compositions, and recycled textiles.

> *"This is what we're focused on: to create a fabric that is fresh and that you don't need to wash as often…"*

To keep in line with the core value of sustainability, INDUO analyses environmental issues from multiple perspectives before deciding which course of action the company will take, Guesné says. "The big problem with [the] environment is there is not one simple factor", she adds. Currently, they are conducting an independent study to analyse the fabric's overall impact on the environment. As part of the study, researchers are trying to determine whether it is more sustainable for the brand to use conventional cotton or organic cotton. To Guesné's surprise, the question is more complex than she would have assumed – making one shirt from organic cotton requires twice as much field space than conventional cotton, she says. "Yes, cotton is not the perfect environmental solution, but if you make it a little bit more environmentally friendly with technology, that's a plus", she concludes. While they are analysing other options, the founder stresses that cotton is a very important fibre in the European market – for men, it's the third most important criteria when it comes to buying clothes, after price and style.

Company officials must replicate this balancing act with every production step, considering the amount of energy and water they use, chemical toxicity, material transportation, garment durability, and recycling potential. Because there are so many steps required to produce the fabric, making the production cycle longer – four months instead of two – INDUO does consume more energy and water, Guesné admits. But ultimately, she asserts that it is insignificant compared to the environmental gains provided by the fabric's lifetime durability.

Photo: Frédéric Baron-Morin

### ▶ CARE ADVICE

INDUO highly values customer experience and wants to make sure that all their products are easy to incorporate into daily habits, the company founder says. While the fabric is water-resistant it is not waterproof, which means that it is completely washing-machine friendly. She assured us that the garments can be washed and ironed normally, following the normal care instructions for conventional cotton materials.

# KAPOK

Gianni Versace once said, "I am not interested in the past, except as the road to the future". Taking Versace's words to heart, Flocus, a Dutch company, is looking to pave the way to the future by using a fibre of the past: kapok. Kapok's cotton-like fibres, found in the tree's seed pods, were very popular for use in mattresses and pillows in our grandparents' time, but have slowly been forgotten with the development of synthetic materials. Flocus is the first company to bring the fashion industry's attention back to kapok and explore its many uses as a solution to the industry's reliance on non-renewable fossil fuels in textile production.

"Flocus has chosen to work with kapok fibre because it's a remarkable fibre from a functional point of view, but also from that of sustainability", explains co-founder and co-owner Jeroen Muijsers. These fibres can deceive the senses, as they look and feel a little like cotton fibres. The resulting textiles made from kapok are dry and breezy, with a cotton-silk touch – yet they are also insulating and incredibly good at temperature regulation, Muijsers says. These "remarkable" fibres differ from cotton in one key aspect: sustainability. The tree requires no fertilizers, irrigation or pesticides to grow, and the production process uses minimal quantities of water and energy, and no chemicals, making kapok a "pure product", he continues. Muijsers began working with these tropical fibres around six years ago, when his work as a commercial textile engineer led him to a Chinese kapok supplier. In one decisive meeting, the supplier showed him some kapok yarns and materials, but told Muijsers that she did not know how to introduce the fibre into the market. From that moment on, Muijsers was hooked on the idea – he "started to learn and dig into kapok, and then it was amazing", he describes. "Sometimes, you know when things come on to your – let's say path – you immediately feel [that] this is the right thing to do".

His extensive career spans 20 years and multiple visits to production countries like Bangladesh and China, during which he encountered a wide spectrum of environmental impacts coming from various production aspects of the textile industry. The discovery of the tropical ingredient drives the new wave of effort to innovate textiles with huge unexplored potential. Muijsers recalls the fact that "very few people knew kapok" when he started to introduce it into the market. There are almost "two, three generations [which] have forgotten these fibres", – supporting his ambition to share his new knowledge about this innovative product with the textile industry and its end customers. Today, Flocus is an ingredient brand that provides raw kapok fibres, but it also supplies fabrics, yarns and other spun fibres to designers around the world. "We are more a vertical solution provider and we work with a lot of partners in the chain", he says.

Flocus is undergoing the Lifecycle assessment to measure the environmental impact of the fibre and the tree itself. At the moment, the only impact the fibre has, as Muijsers states, is the transportation of the pods to the sorting facilities and the mechanical energy used during the cleaning process. The tree provides multiple benefits to the environment, especially since its fibres can be obtained without cutting the tree in any way, unlike other plant-based fibres such as lyocell, he says.

## PRODUCTION JOURNEY

Measuring up to 73 meters tall and 3 meters wide, the kapok tree, also known as Java cotton, ceiba or Java kapok, is a magnificent tree found exclusively in tropical areas, such as Mexico, Central America, the Caribbean, southern Asia and the East Indies, which is where Flocus sources its fibres. There are multiple varieties, not all of which are suitable for creating fibres that can be transformed into apparel. Kapok trees grow differently than most of the other sources for bio-based fibres, setting the fibre apart from any other, Muijsers says. Astonishingly, they only take about six years to grow and start producing the pods where the fibre is located, Muijsers says, requiring only sun, groundwater and lots of rain. Unlike many crops, Kapok trees do not need agricultural land – they can grow on rolling hills, on dark, rich, volcanic soil, and anything in between.

The fibres are found in the tree's oblong, hard-shelled pods that sprout from its branches before flowering, when the tree transforms from a lively green to a bright pink. The pods are either picked from the branches like fruit, or collected from the ground after they've fallen, and are broken open to reveal the white, fluffy fibres that will be spun into high-quality textiles. These fibres are usually hand-cleaned by diligent workers to separate them from the small seeds they protect using a labour-intensive process that Flocus is trying to automate for increased efficiency. Once cleaned, the fibres are transported to the sorting facilities and processed by a machine, creating the long-lasting fibres that are sent to the spinning mill to be spun into yarn, in a process similar to that of cotton production. Here kapok poses its biggest challenge to producers: its short length and extremely light weight make it difficult to spin into yarn, Muijsers says. In his opinion, the benefits outweigh the costs, because the final product is five times lighter than cotton.

The fibres are then blended with other high-performance fibres, such as recycled polyester, wool, organic cotton, and lyocell. These blends allow for the diversity of kapok products; whereas some blends create textiles perfect for yoga or jogging clothes, others are better suited for the fashion industry in general. For now, the blends used to create fashion textiles range from 20 to 30 percent kapok. The brand is still investigating how to create a textile that is 100 percent kapok – which is currently not possible. Its most concentrated blend is 70 percent pure kapok and used for insulation, Muijsers says. Once the fibre is spun, blended and ready to use, it's dyed in the same way most cotton textiles are dyed, since both are cellulose-based fibres. Researchers have found that kapok responds well to both conventional dyes and natural ones extracted from herbs, roots, leaves, and nuts.

## VALUE OF THE FABRIC

Many people tend to compare cotton with kapok, since they have similar qualities and the finished kapok yarn has a cotton-silk touch. Nevertheless, Muijsers stresses that there are many notable differences between these fibres. For one, cotton requires extensive certifications to prove that it has been sourced in an ethical, organic way, such as the GOTS certificate, because most cotton is not produced organically. Kapok, on the other hand, grows organically, which means there is no differentiation between non-organic kapok and organic kapok, and therefore it does not need additional certification, Muijsers explains. He also makes the point that cotton is a high-impact crop, whereas kapok is one of the lowest impact crops, as it not only grows organically and helps reforestation efforts, but also stores large amounts of carbon, nitrogen, and other toxic gases. Kapok harvesting empowers local farmers and gives them the option to start poly-cropping with corn, peppers or vanilla to diversify their incomes, he continues. The fibre is also hollow, which is why it's an effective heat insulator, perfect for use in down jackets, blankets, pillows, and mattresses, Muijsers says. Kapok's strength lies in its temperature-regulating qualities, as it's both breathable and insulating, making it great for top-of-the line sportswear and active clothes. Kapok blends imbue the fabrics with many characteristics. Its blend with recycled polyester creates an ideal combination for use in sportswear since Flocus' ingredient enhances the value and function of the finished textiles, giving them a "more natural feel", Muijsers states. "You don't really notice the synthetic part", he continues, referring to the recycled polyester blend. The component would naturally regulate your body temperature and you wouldn't sweat as much as with 100 percent polyester garments which have less breathability.

> *"Kapok's hydrophobic properties make it drier and softer than cotton and other fibres, but it still feels comfortable, as it repels water; it's also anti-bacterial and hypoallergenic".*

Kapok's hydrophobic properties make it drier and softer than cotton and other fibres, but it still feels comfortable, as it repels water; it's also antibacterial and hypoallergenic. "It's a natural fibre with so many properties that it performs like synthetic fibres", Muijsers says excitedly. Synthetic fibres could easily be replaced with kapok ones, giving the finished textiles the same qualities and making them vegan with a naturally based fibre. The fibre's biggest contribution to the textile industry is the expansion of eco-friendly fibre options, of which there are currently not enough, Muijsers says. There are not enough organic cotton supplies on the market to fill up designers' collections, and using other fibres would give clothes a different feel, so using kapok – which is organic and has a smoother and silkier feel than cotton – is quite an attractive alternative. Because the fibre has been slowly forgotten as a relic of the past, there have been relatively few agricultural initiatives to greatly increase its supply, but there is a little research on the kapok industry that allows for rough estimates of its relevance in the market. Muijsers guesses, based on official resources and personal experience, that there is currently as much kapok as organic cotton on the market, approximately 120 million kilos per year. He also believes that as the demand for kapok as a sustainable fibre increases, there can be a kapok reforestation initiative that will contribute to Flocus' positive impact on the planet. "We can plant more trees and have a good product [...] to be used in materials with lower impact", he says. To maximize the fibre's potential, there needs to be increased awareness of its benefits among consumers and designers, he continues. By scaling up, Muijsers also hopes that they can lower the price of the fibres. Currently, kapok is more expensive than cotton, partly due to the difference in market demands, but also because it still requires a significant amount of manual labour to produce.

Because of its various properties, kapok can be used in different markets and applications, including sportswear, home textiles, and the car industry. In Muijsers's experience, sportswear brands have been the most advanced industry and the first to adopt more sustainable solutions like kapok fibre. Flocus' first customer was Protective, a German bike wear company that developed cycling shorts and insulated jackets with the Flocus fibre – and the feedback they have received has been overwhelmingly positive, allowing the brand to help reduce the use of fossil fuel-based materials in the market, he says. "We are very happy to see that a lot of brands are becoming more ethical in how they buy", he continues. "Because at the end [...] nobody can be perfect from day one, but if they say, 'Hey, we are going to take these steps to become more sustainable,' those are the companies we would like to cooperate with and grow together".

▶ **CARE ADVICE**

The care instructions for kapok garments are the same as those for cotton clothes, Muijsers says. In the Dutch entrepreneur's opinion, it's generally good to wash clothes at between 30 to 40 degrees to save energy. To prevent shrinking, avoid over-drying garments in the dryer, or simply line dry them.

Photo: Flocus

# NATURAL FIBRES

TINTEX is yet another manufacturer that is forging its path as a green solution. This Portuguese company took a good, long look at cotton production and pinpointed a brand new strategy to make it more efficient. Twenty years after establishing itself as a quality dyer and finisher, the company is now recognized for replacing conventional cotton and developing a responsible textile line made of naturally advanced yarns which incorporate cutting-edge, sustainable knitting technology.

Forty percent of TINTEX textiles are made from organic, GOTS certified cotton; another 40 percent uses TENCEL™ Lyocell, Modal, and Micromodal, and the remaining 20 percent relies on other smart materials like Bemberg™ by Asahi Kasei, Seacell, or natural linens, explains TINTEX's Communication Assistant, Camilla Carrara. "Natural fibres, and in particular, a new generation of smart cottons, represent one of the key assets of TINTEX", she continues. "It embodies the essence of our Naturally Advanced concept". Most of the fabrics are blended to create special qualities, and their versatility has made them increasingly popular within the fashion industry. They can be used for making anything – from nightwear and lingerie to outerwear and sportswear, depending on the dyeing and finishing processes, she adds.

## RESPONSIBLE COTTON

Today's brands are looking for contemporary design, innovation and sustainability, and TINTEX is in the perfect position to satisfy their needs, Carrara says. They offer three premium, advanced cotton solutions: ECOTEC® by Marchi & Fildi, GOTS cotton, and Supima cotton. ECOTEC® is innovative cotton made from post-consumer cuts that saves up to 77.9 percent of the water consumed in the conventional cotton production process. GOTS (Global Organic Textile Standard)- certified cotton ensures traceability, sustainability, and positive social impact throughout the entire supply chain. It's imperative to establish trust between TINTEX and its consumers, allowing the brand to have sustainable growth by boosting their reputation and corporate identity. Premium brands can also use Supima cotton, whose extra-long American fibres create luxury textiles for anything from quality cashmeres to other high-end garments.

## IMPROVING DYEING + ENVIRONMENTAL IMPACT

TINTEX has collaborated with multiple partners, like ColorZen®, Tearfil Textile Yarns, and Becri Group to elevate its collection to the apex of creativity and performance. Through collaborative experimentation, they are aiming to make the cotton dyeing process more efficient and sustainable by reducing water use and eliminating up to 95 percent of toxic chemicals. According to Carrara, TINTEX guarantees up to a 70 percent improvement in environmental impact with their production processes. They have reduced water, gas, and energy consumption, as well as minimized their use of toxic chemicals. The brand's waste management processes can recycle or reuse 98 percent of all production waste, and most of their energy is collected by photovoltaic panels and solar energy systems.

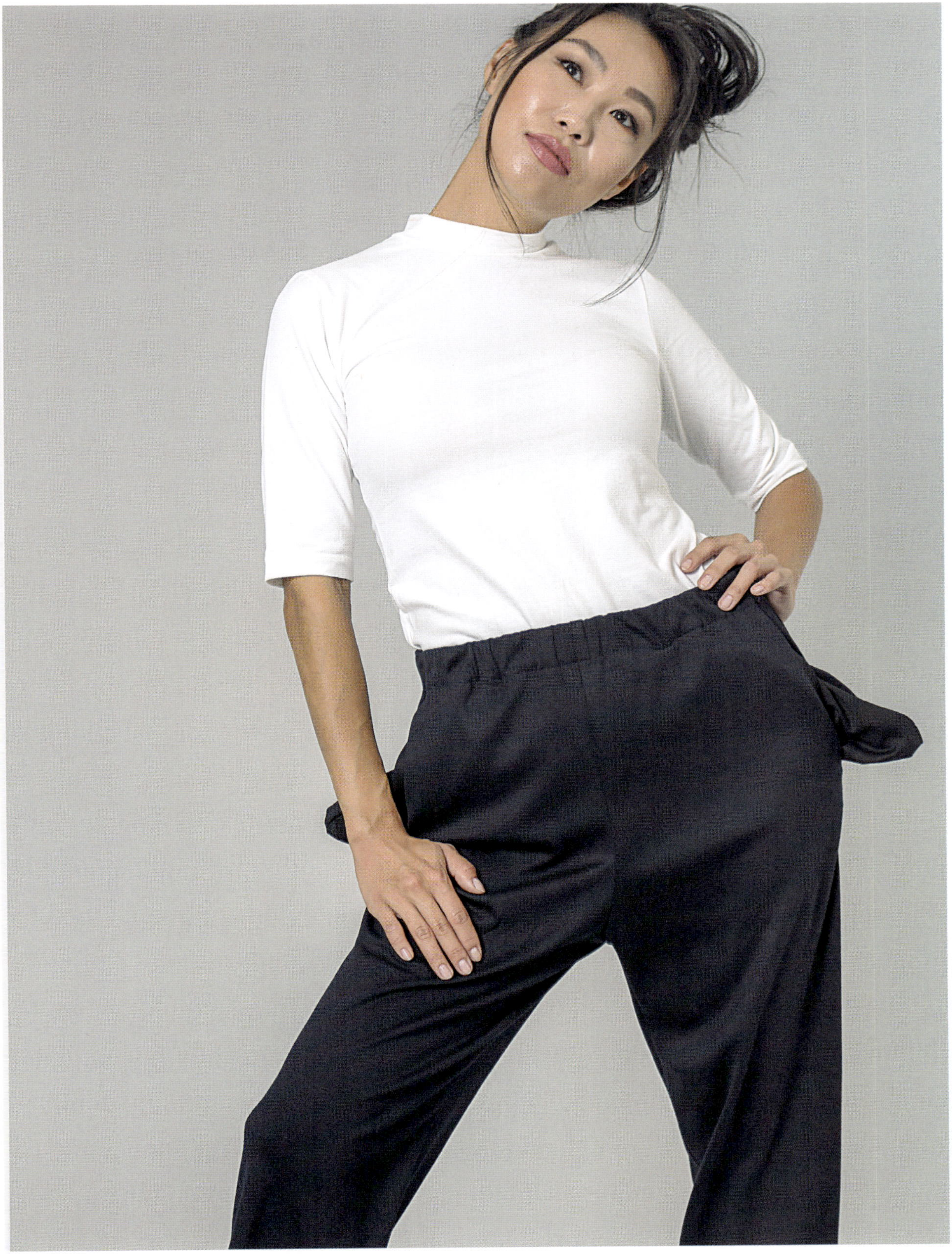

*"Our role is to provide brands and retailers with a full [description] of [our] values [with] each [...] product: contemporary design plus innovation plus sustainability, all in one".*

## VALUE OF FINISHES

One of TINTEX's major milestones has been creating their unique finishing process called Naturally Clean®, which launched in September 2018 and targets cellulosic fibres. "Naturally Clean takes a cost-effective, modern approach that eliminates aggressive treatments and optimizes clean surfaces, vivid colours, and a beautiful smooth-to-the-touch feel", Carrara writes. This technology maintains the textile's original characteristics for an extended amount of time, while using Oeko-Tex – and, in the future, bluesign® – certified chemicals. While not all fibres can be finished using Naturally Clean® technology, the process can be applied to most of TINTEX's cotton products. A few brands, including the well-known Nordic brand, Filippa K, have already adopted it as their go-to finishing process.

While working with Filippa K, TINTEX brand representatives crafted a thoughtful, effective communication method that set the precedent for their client interactions. "We do not see ourselves just as suppliers, but really as partners", Carrara explains. Their approach has proved effective, as the brand expects a 30 percent growth spurt by the end of 2020. Regardless, there are still several obstacles in the market that must be navigated. In Carrara's opinion, there is the misconception that sustainable fashion does not look as good as conventional fashion, but consumers are rapidly evolving and want to have access to information about the values that have guided the production of their garments. "Our role is to provide brands and retailers with a full [description] of [our] values [with] each [...] product: contemporary design plus innovation plus sustainability, all in one", she writes.

# VISCOSE, MODAL, TENCEL

Cellulose-based fibres, and viscose among them, are the third most used after polyester and cotton in the fibre market. Being the most used fibres, it is expected their demand will increase, with estimates that the consumption of garments made with them will grow by 8,5% by 2030, and viscose alone will increase by 5% per annum until 2023. This outlook for the future of textiles suggests an absolute need for production companies to put an emphasis on reviewing current business models and consumption patterns in order to move towards more sustainable practices. While cellulosic fibres themselves are not toxic or polluting, conventional production methods can have detrimental effects on the environment, workers and local communities – especially in the case of viscose and modal. Viscose, for instance, is traditionally produced by treating wood pulp with highly toxic chemicals that are released into the atmosphere and pose serious health hazards, not just for the factory workers but for families living near the production plants. The Changing Markets Foundation have become a catalyst for change within the global viscose industry, reporting pressing problems in India, Indonesia and China as noted in The Dirty Fashion Report. A 2017 investigation, for instance, found that Chinese viscose companies, accounting for 63 percent of global production, deliberately violated government regulations by dumping toxic chemicals into lakes, oceans, and other waterways. In addition, its production speeds up deforestation, as forests are cleared to make way for fast-growing trees, like bamboo and eucalyptus used to produce pulp. To make viscose and modal truly sustainable fibres, leading world producers need to upgrade the conventional roadmap for sourcing and production processes by investing in closed-loop systems with proper standardized regulations and a set of sustainable measurements. The Austrian company Lenzing, the world's second largest cellulose fibre manufacturer, with operations spanning throughout Europe, Asia and North America, is an example of these positive changes. Their viscose, modal and lyocell production is providing sustainable alternatives to their conventional counterparts, which have been criticized for their high environmental impact.

## THE FIBRES

Viscose is the oldest of the three fibres, invented in the late 1800s by French scientist, Hilaire de Chardonnet. Lenzing jumped on the viscose-producing bandwagon in 1936, keeping their eyes peeled for future innovation opportunities. One presented itself with the Japanese invention of modal in 1951, which the company began producing in the 1960s, while two decades later, micromodal, a softer version of modal, was introduced. In 1992, with the development of technology, the company introduced TENCEL™ Lyocell in Mobile, Alabama, its United States operations plant, making it a more sustainable option than viscose. ECOVERO™ looks to address sustainability issues by presenting an eco-friendly viscose option. The trees used to make these fibres are sourced from sustainably managed forests that are either Forest Stewardship Council or Program for Endorsement of Forest Certification Scheme approved. Also, the company's European operations plants in Austria and the Czech Republic obtain their wood – beech, spruce and birch – from approved Central European forests. Additionally, Lenzing TENCEL™ Lyocell and Modal are produced with ethically sourced wood, and the company collaborates with CanopyStyle's reforestation efforts.

## PRODUCTION JOURNEY

Conventional viscose production wastes approximately 70 percent of the tree, but Lenzing's European biorefineries maximize the use of this precious natural resource and reduce waste as much as possible. The company makes all their fibres using their own energy to reduce excess carbon emissions, and their processes are a "closed-loop production", meaning that there is a modern chemical management system and little waste. When pulp is transformed into viscose or modal, sodium sulphate and a sweetener are produced as co-products. Instead of letting them go to waste, and in order to propel a circular economy, Lenzing sells them to companies to be used as a foundation for detergents, dyes, powders, industrial chemicals, sugar and other sweeteners. As for lyocell fibres, there are no co-products because the company is able to recover up to 99 percent of the solvent they use, which creates a clean production loop. Once obtained from the trees, all the fibres then undergo extensive mechanical and chemical processes, including flattening, immersions in caustic soda, spinning and finishing, until the final product is made into yarns. Lenzing has an additional line of TENCEL™ Lyocell fibres that are produced with their innovative REFIBRA™ technology, created as part of their effort to close the loop in the fashion industry. To make REFIBRA™ fibres, the company obtains pre-consumer cotton cutting waste from garment manufacturers and breaks it down to create recycled cotton fibres. These are then mixed into wood pulp to create new TENCEL™ Lyocell.

## VALUE OF THE FABRIC

These fibres have soft, breathable and great absorbing moisture properties. They have excellent colour retention and vibrancy, with a similar touch to cotton, making them a great alternative to use for clothes that are in contact with skin. They can also be blended with other fibres, like cotton and spandex, to enhance their beneficial properties. TENCEL™ Lyocell has been used in denim, intimate apparel, footwear, sportswear, home textiles and furniture, and is especially popular for t-shirts and other soft apparel items. Modal and Micro Modal® are silkier and finer, and are often used in intimate apparel, underwear and home wear, while viscose is best for linings, coats, pants, shirts, jackets and other outerwear. Garments made with these fibres are biodegradable and compostable in marine and soil conditions. The fibres' compostability, though, depends on the blend type and finishing process, since these factors can slow down biodegradation. Luckily there are currently multiple research projects focused on eliminating these hindrances and improving the fibres' biodegradation in different environments. The production for TENCEL™ Lyocell fibres has received the European Award for the Environment from the European Commission, and all three products consistently rank low in the Higg index for the company's European-made fibres. Lyocell has a Higg index of 57, modal 67, and viscose has a score of 62. In contrast, conventional cotton has a Higg index of 98. These rankings are specific to the fibres produced in the Lenzing plant.

Lenzing Austria and Czech Republic have their own pulp dissolving mills that reduce wood and chemical waste. The Asian fibres have higher scores because there is no pulp plant in Asia, limiting some of the ecological benefits of the fibre production. After the company's Indonesian South Pacific Viscose fibres plant was featured in the Dirty Fashion report in 2017, Lenzing voluntarily set up an action plan to innovate the factory by implementing a "closed-loop" process aimed at reducing significant pollution by 2022. While much progress remains to be made, the tide is beginning to turn in favour of more responsible viscose production. Once brands and retailers start to appreciate the value of sustainable fibres, tracing their origin and its production process, customers will have more garments designed in a responsible way.

▶ **CARE ADVICE**

Cellulose-based fibres can be cared for in the same way as a cotton fabric. They can be washed, ironed, and dried. Any special instructions particular to the garment should be followed, in the same way that a fine cotton garment should be treated, following specific care instructions.

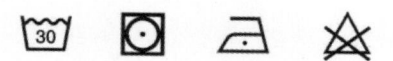

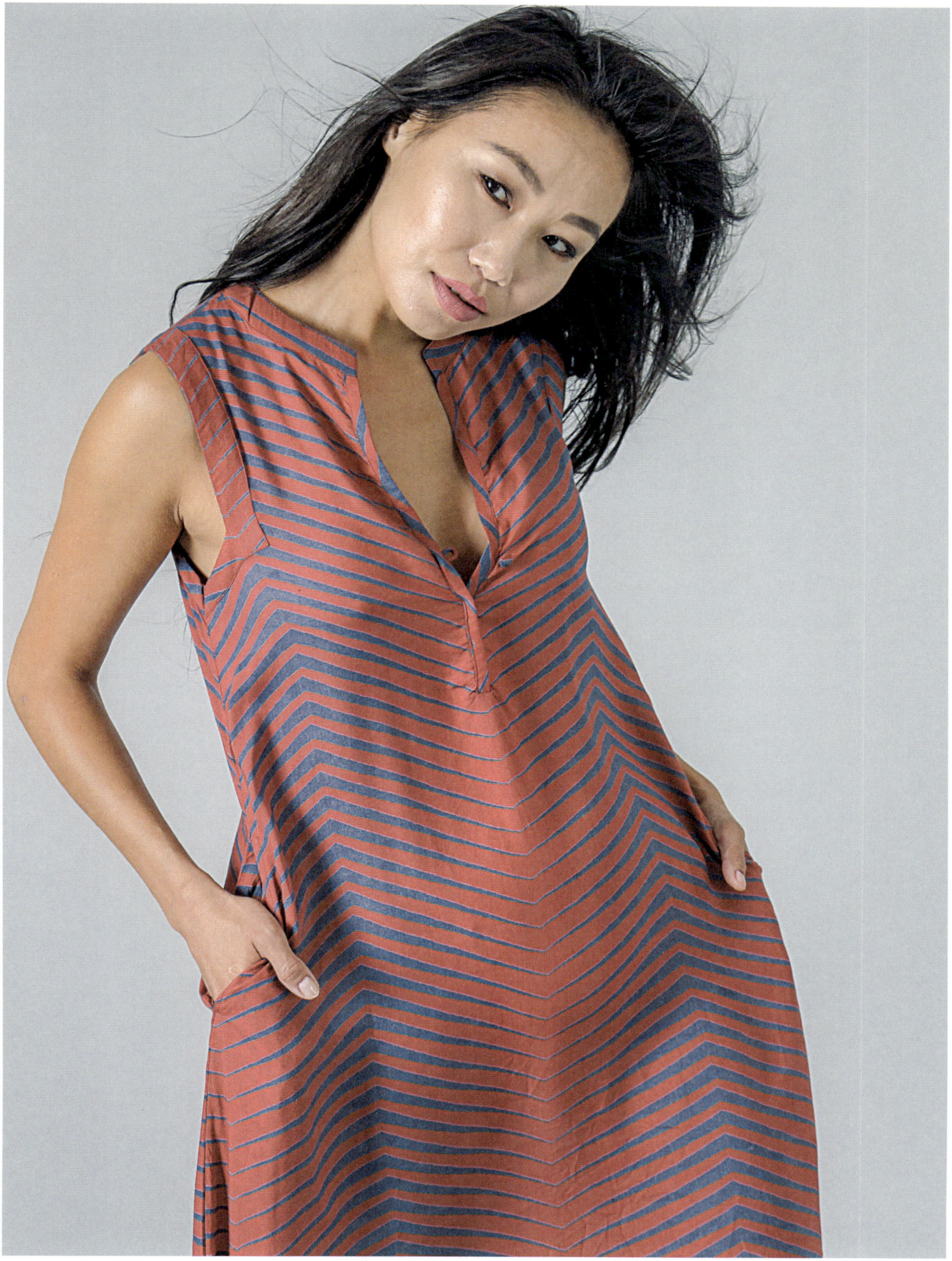

# RECYCLED DENIM

You no longer have to fight off feelings of guilt and nostalgia as you throw away your favourite pair of worn-out jeans; you can rest assured that they have found a way to reincarnate them as something better. Recover®, a company based in Spain, has spent 73 years perfecting a process of recycling used denim and other wasted cotton textiles and repurposing them into brand new clothes.

In the mid-1940s, Spain was undergoing significant political turmoil, as the country dealt with the devastating economic repercussions of World War II and the Spanish Civil War. At the time, the Ferrer family, which now owns and runs Recover, produced and distributed fertilizer, as well as the cotton sacks to package the fertilizer. The period of scarcity affected them harshly, as they struggled to obtain the cotton needed to produce the sacks, until they realized they could recycle the fibres from old, torn sacks. Over the years they evolved from creating new sacks, to "down-cycling" the yarns for mops and wipers, to finally developing today's performance products, Paqui Ferrer, Recover® marketing director, explains.

"They had to be very creative because they had no other choice", she says. In the past, technology only allowed for the production of these recycled, low-end products, but with expertise and constant development, Recover® engineered an effective process that creates attractive, high-end fabrics for the highly desired and lucrative fashion segment. Today, they are basically able to make any kind of textile product with their recycled yarn, which is so good that there is no difference between the recycled fibres and the conventional ones.

Recover's remarkable process allows for the creation of premium yarns in 300 different colours and textures, without the need for dyes, water, or high

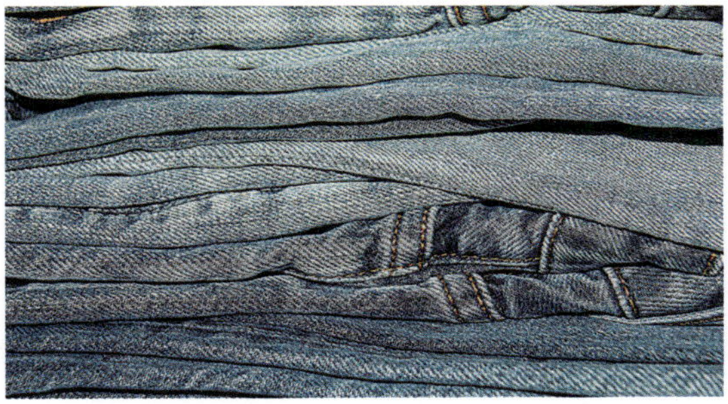
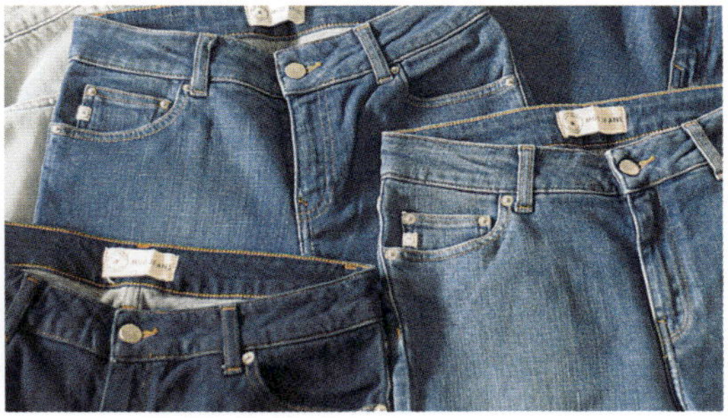
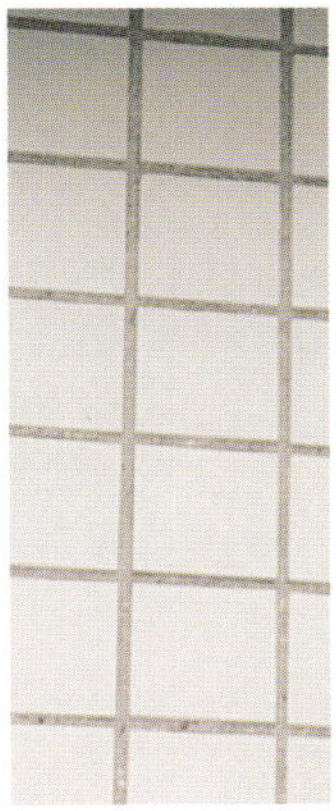
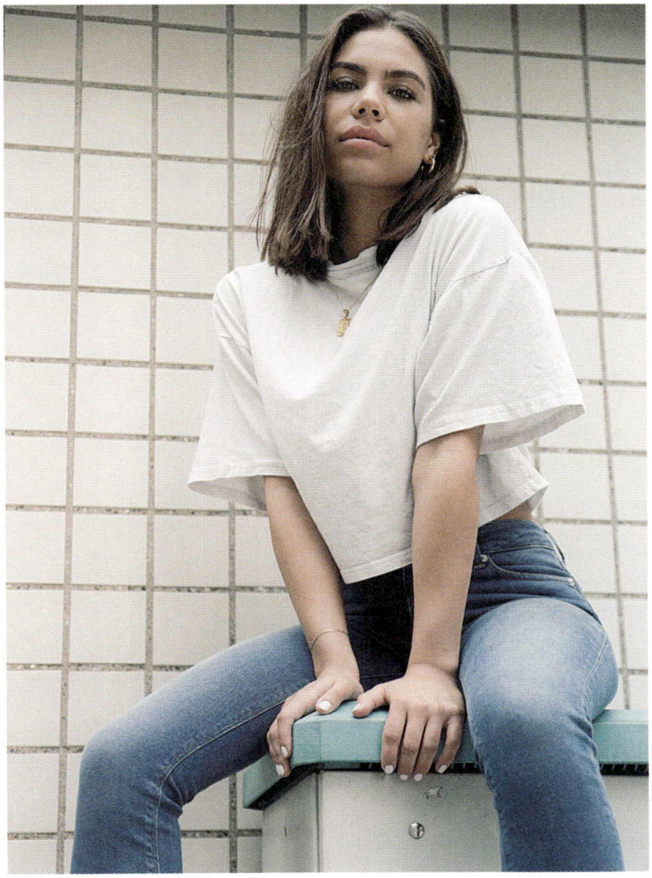
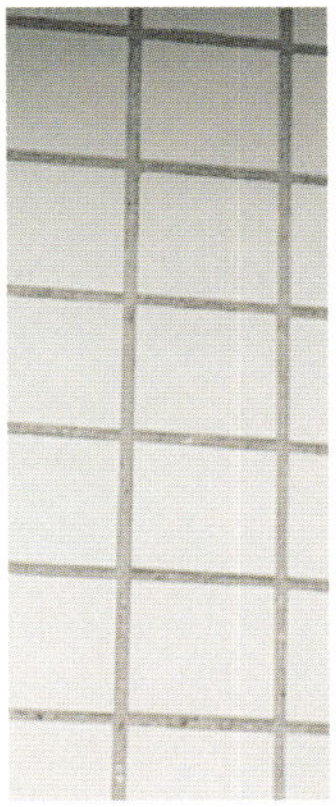
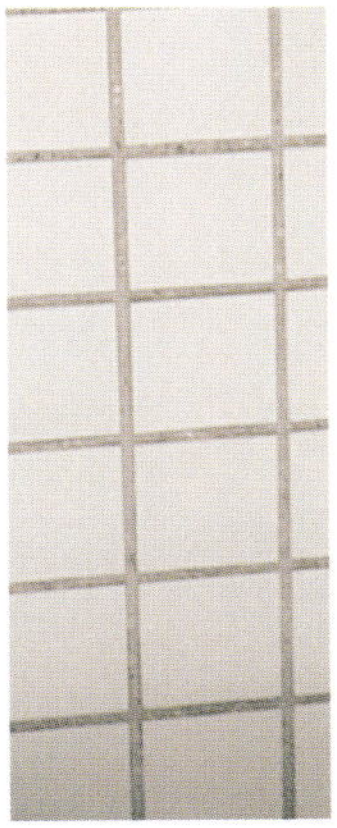
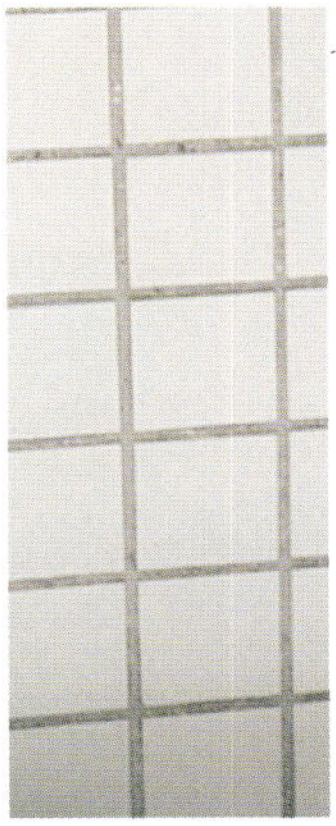
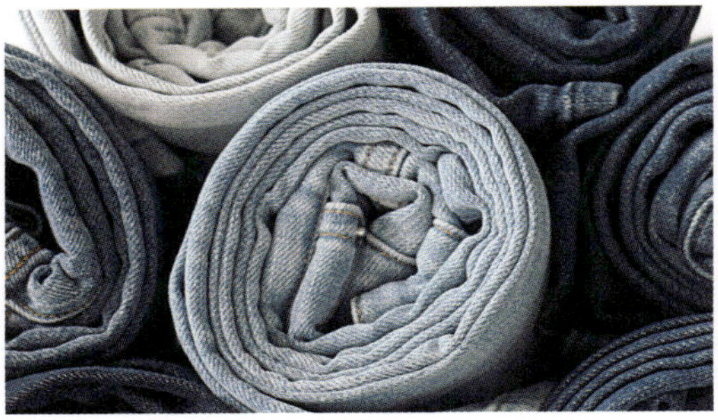
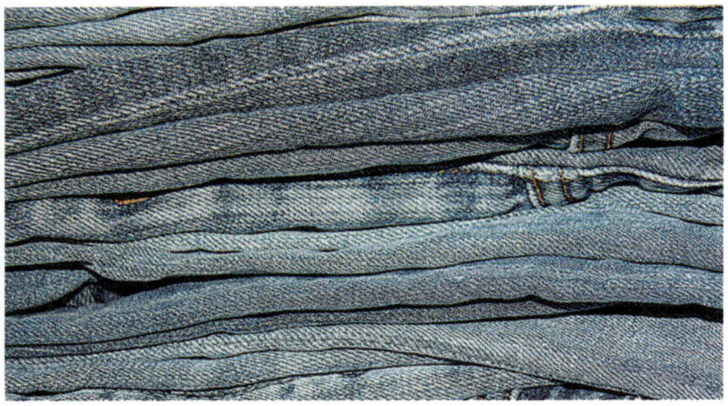

levels of energy. The company's only raw materials are waste textiles, providing an attractive solution for textiles with high environmental impacts, such as denim. Recover Jeans(™) is one of the company's most popular ranges, with high profile clients such as Tommy Hilfiger, G-Star Raw, Bonobo Jeans and Wrangler.

The denim industry's environmental footprint has constantly faced criticism from sustainability advocates. The process consumes large amounts of energy and water — about 8,000 litres of water are used to produce a single pair of jeans - from the water needed to grow the cotton to the dyeing and production, explains Ferrer. Moreover, the indigo dyes and bleaches used to give jeans their finishing touches, like the stone wash, use dangerous chemicals which, if not treated correctly – and most aren't – can contaminate rivers and oceans. "What we have done with the denim industry is create a circular solution that doesn't add more pressure to the environment", she says. What Recover® fibres can achieve doesn't just stop at recycled denim. The refurbished cotton yarns can be used for anything, including shoes, clothes, knitting, accessories, bags, socks, curtains, upholstery and other home decor items. Ferrer asserts that after 73 years of experience, the company really knows what to do with recycled fibres – and they keep trying to improve their processes to reduce their environmental impact.

## PRODUCTION JOURNEY

Before Recover® can breathe new life into used garments, they need to obtain the most crucial ingredient: used, recyclable textiles. Ninety percent of their raw material is sourced from pre-industrial waste, which is the textile waste produced by large industrial hubs all over the world. The rest is obtained from post-consumer waste, which is used clothes people discard. Most of Recover's denim fabrication comes from the latter, as they buy used jeans from a Spanish non-profit organization that collects denim unsuitable for the second-hand channel from shops around the country and removes labels, buttons, and zips. "We have two resources: the post-consumer denim is more from a social source and the other has to be from big industrial hubs because they are the ones producing the waste", Ferrer says. Both sources are sorted based on colour and quality, and then transferred to the company's mechanical processing centre, where the cotton is recycled.

*"We have two resources: the postconsumer denim is more from a social source and the other has to be from big industrial hubs because they are the ones producing the waste..."*

Today's up-cycling system is comprised of two main processes that jeans and textile waste have to undergo before they can be reborn: fibre upcycling and colour blending. In fibre upcycling, which is how they recycle cotton, the textiles are cut into tiny pieces and processed by a machine they call "El Diablo". This machine extracts the fibre from the fabrics, while preserving their length and quality. Once the fibre is recovered, it's sent to "the kitchen" where similarly coloured fibres are blended to create precise and unique colours.

"The cotton waste that we recycle always comes in colours, like black, blue, red, yellow, etc. This means that we don't need to dye", Ferrer explains. Recover's processes are scalable: they are used for the mass production of fibres. In the final step, the recovered fibres are spun into low-impact, premium yarns, ready to begin a new life.

Recover's special denim line, Recover Jeans, undergoes a similar production process, with a few slight changes. During the blending process, the used cotton fibres are mixed with organic cotton, producing ready-to-wear denim and creating a "closed loop solution" for turning an old pair of jeans into a brand new pair. According to Ferrer, the denim waste can be recycled somewhere between two and three times – for now. In the future, there is the potential to recycle it many more times. Recover® has developed a special partnership with one denim brand to make jeans out of 100 percent recycled material, compatible with the brand's innovative foam dyeing process, an eco-friendly way to dye jeans.

The masterminds behind the Recover® process have perfected it to the extent that the company can offer a wide range of products tailored to designers' needs. These include Recover Tech, which is geared towards sportswear; Recover 3, which includes Tencel for a softer touch; and their bestseller, Recover Blue, which includes fibres from recycled PET bottles as well as cotton, among other lines. The search for sustainability doesn't stop there, as the brand continues to experiment with different fibres and raw materials to expand their offerings. Their engineers have already created a new line, Recover Wool, which uses recycled wool instead of cotton, and they are working on recycling viscose and rayon. "I think there is no limit for the time being", Ferrer answers when asked about the future of Recover research,

Photo: Mud Jeans

"there are many, many products that we can recycle and there is a lot to be discovered in this field".

## VALUE OF THE FABRIC

Perhaps the most astounding thing about Recover Jeans and their fabrics is that "you cannot tell the difference by touching it", especially when compared to conventional cotton, Ferrer says. Brands who want to switch over to a sustainable alternative no longer have to worry about sacrificing quality, as Recover® provides quality and sustainability wrapped together. For example, Tommy Hilfiger has produced jeans made with recovered post-industrial cotton waste, and G-Star RAW has produced denim made with recycled post-consumer garments. "When you look at them [...], you would never tell that these are made out of recycled material", Ferrer says proudly.

Thanks to Recover's high levels of traceability, customers can now increasingly be aware of the exact impact their newly purchased shirt, dress or jeans has had on the environment. In Recover's case, the effects are overwhelmingly positive – in 2018 alone, the company's yarns saved a whopping 43.4 billion litres of water, 3.2 million kilograms of pollutants, 157 million kilowatts of energy, 2.9 million kilograms of textile waste, and 61 million kilograms of carbon dioxide emissions. Recover® cotton also has the benefit of being the lowest-impact cotton fibre on the global market, according to the Higg Material Sustainability Index. Conventional cotton has a score of 76.5; by contrast, Recover® cotton fibres have a score of 8, proving that it is an amazing sustainable alternative to high-impact materials. Ferrer believes that the textiles' sustainability, combined with Recover's seven decades of experience, are the company's strongest selling points. The biggest challenge has been changing the mindsets of brands and consumers. Sustainable products have been market-available for years, but recycled clothes are a new, innovative concept that may be hard to grasp for many, since brands are afraid that the customer may not accept the clothes' recycled origin. To Ferrer, it seems that the brands are all watching each other to see who takes the first leap of faith and presents a recycled collection. "The customer is ready for that and ready to pay a little bit extra for these garments", especially Millennials and Generation Z's, she says. "We see it every day on the news, the young are the ones who are really fighting [for] this", she says — but she stresses that recyclable fashion could be adopted by all generations. Recover has already collaborated with Weekday, a brand that is part of the H&M group, to provide their recycled fibres for a capsule collection. And this group didn't just want sustainable, or organic materials, they clearly stated they wanted recycled fibres, Ferrer says, showing that the market is more than ready to look towards a recycled future.

▶ **CARE ADVICE**

In the same way that Recover® yarns don't feel or look any different to conventional cotton yarns, there is no difference in the care instructions, Ferrer assures us. Most cotton garments are easily washed at home, but checking the garment's individual care instructions is a must before throwing it into the washing machine. It's best to wash most cotton clothes with warm or cold water on the normal or gentle cycle. To prevent your favourite shirt or slacks from shrinking, avoid over-drying the garments in the dryer and use a lower temperature or a shorter drying time — or hang the garments out to dry. If the clothes are taken out of the dryer and immediately folded, odds are you won't have to iron them, as cotton doesn't wrinkle as easily as other fabrics. In the case that wrinkling does occur, use a medium hot iron on the reverse side of the fabric.

Care instructions for denim vary slightly, as there are certain golden rules that should be followed to preserve jeans as long as possible. First, they shouldn't be washed all that often — experts recommend washing them after five to ten wears, depending on individual conditions. Second, don't throw them in the dryer! Line drying helps preserve the jeans' shape and fit and helps them last longer. Lastly, wash denim in cold water to keep the dye intact. Striving to make your jeans last longer is another small step you can take to help the environment, as it requires buying fewer items — and buying better items. And before throwing that old pair of jeans into the bin, "just think, it can become a new product that can be used by somebody else", Ferrer advises.

# CASE STUDY: PANAMA TRIMMINGS—LABELS

Panama Trimmings, an Italian label-making company, had great foresight into the denim market's future potential and capitalized on its weakest link – the creative community's lack of options in sustainable labels that can add value to a brand's autograph. The first step in widening the sustainable assortment of labels has taken seven years, as the company developed high-quality recycled labels that astonish its customer base with hundreds of customizable designs, Angela Zen, area sales manager at Panama Trimmings, says. Many of Panama Trimming's customers have been forced to switch to sustainable labels, while others have been motivated by their values to give sustainable materials a chance. Recycled leather labels were one of the first sustainable trimming lines introduced. In Zen's opinion this did not turn out too well as there was not enough aesthetic charm. "What's important to highlight, as a successful formula to launch a sustainable product, is interest in sustainable products from customers, a good price point and aesthetic", Zen says about Panama Trimming's formula for success.

Learning quickly from their experiences, company researchers developed superior alternatives that have become their most popular products. According to Zen, 70 to 80 percent of their customers are ready to buy sustainable trimmings, especially since the company's researchers have poured their hearts and souls into making attractive, high-quality sustainable alternatives. As a result, for the upcoming autumn and winter 20/21 seasons, recycled content is the biggest emerging material trend in textiles, Zen says. The sustainable labels decorating denim products worldwide will be produced by the Italian company for clothing labels like Gucci, Lee, Wrangler, H&M, Tiger of Sweden, Max Mara and Pierre Cardin, to name a few. In all their years producing trimmings and labels, Panama Trimmings has constantly sought to innovate by conducting extensive in-house research.

Company representatives buy and carefully curate the raw materials used for all collections, testing to ensure everything complies with stringent criteria, and all the energy consumed by the cutting, printing and washing of raw materials comes from the solar panels that line their roofs. Instead of dyeing their products, most are made with water-based ink, which has a lower impact on the environment due to its reduced solvent concentration, Zen explains. While their catalogue is quite extensive, there are five sustainable initiatives that she highlighted from the AW20/21 collection.

## 1. VIRIDIS

Viridis, which means "green" and "last forever" in Latin, is Panama Trimmings newest material, launched in 2018. Viridis is the first polyurethane (PU) leather alternative made from vegetable polyols extracted from corn – yes, the same grain that is cultivated for feeding livestock or producing ethanol and its byproducts. "Just about anything that can be made from a barrel of oil can be made from a bushel of corn and that's why renewable, environmentally-friendly corn is replacing petroleum products", Zen says. Viridis biomass exceeds 75 percent, as the material is made from 48.6 percent corn polyols, 27 percent cotton and 24.4 percent normal PU.

It may be difficult to believe that corn can transform into this leather-like material. The vintage-looking label has a natural pull-up effect and can even be hot printed like genuine leather. True to its name, the material is "very durable", and according to Zen's calculations, Viridis labels will outlive the jeans they are stitched on and are non-biodegradable.

A Life Cycle Assessment (LCA) study* of Viridis found that the material was significantly less damaging to the environment than comparable traditional fossil-fuel products. The study found that Viridis had an improvement contribution of 30 percent for the "Global Warming Potential" impact category, and the "Non-Renewable Energy" category was 50 percent lower.

# *LIFE CYCLE ASSESSMENT (LCA) STUDY OF VIRIDIS

This calculation method displays the results in "millipoints(mPt)" and is an effective tool for designers as it aggregates the results of an LCA in quantities that are easily understandable and usable, called Eco-indicators. This method analyses four different types of damage (endpoints): **Human Health, Ecosystem Quality, Climate Change, and Resource.**

**COMPARISON OF TRADITIONAL PRODUCT (FOSSIL) VS VIRIDIS® PRODUCT (BIO-BASED)**

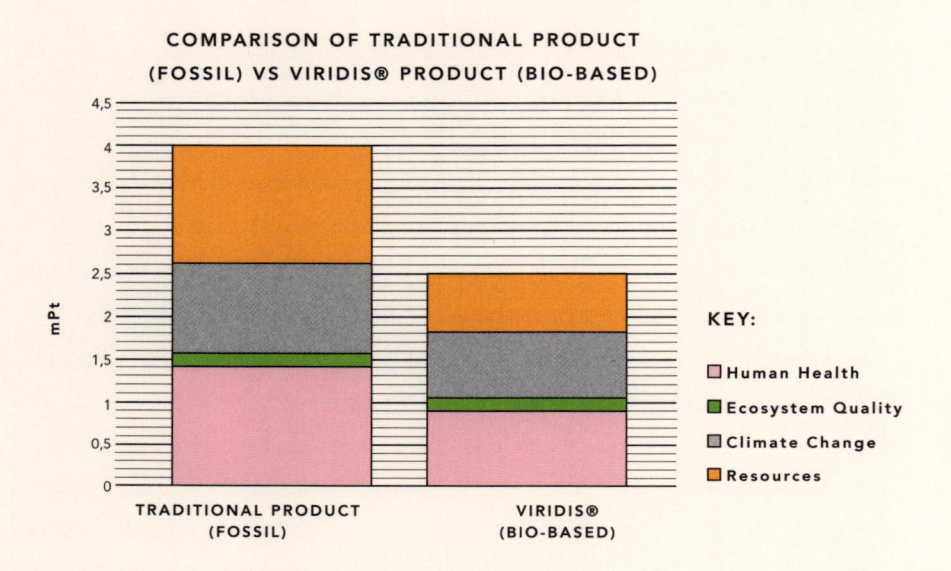

KEY:
- Human Health
- Ecosystem Quality
- Climate Change
- Resources

## 2. CHROME-FREE LEATHER

Using chrome-free leather is another way that the company is responding to the demand for eco-friendly labels. Chrome-free leather is made from a combination of synthetic and vegetable tannins that can help avoid the negative environmental impact produced by conventional chrome tanning mechanisms. This process is similar to vegetable tanning, without the problems that accompany this method: bleeding, shrinking, and long, laborious production hours.

## 3. RECYCLED NYLON

These soft, stylized, fluffy labels are made from Econyl®, a fabric crafted from regenerated nylon derived from recycled post-consumer materials. It's available in a wide array of colours and has an elegant finish that makes it perfect for inside labels, Zen says.

## 4. G- LABEL®: RECYCLED GRAPHITE PRINTING

Graphite is no longer excluded from the fashion industry and confined to being the main component in pencils. Panama Trimmings partnered with a famous pencil brand, Perpetua®, to upcycle wasted graphite powder and use it as a printing method. The company has devised a fool-proof way of collaborating with brands and individual designers to produce a quality product that reflects that brand's identity. From the moment designers choose to create a label, it may take up to two or three seasons before it makes its market debut, Zen discloses. These different label lines can range from "contemporary denim to a more streetwear/fashion look, but you can still find denim heritage and a classic look", she says.

## 5. RECYCLED LEATHER

The company's recycled leather products have greatly improved since its pilot program seven years ago. Today, the labels have significantly improved in look and touch, to the extent that the beautifully crafted products are difficult to tell apart from non-recycled ones. The recycled leather that Panama Trimmings uses is entirely repurposed to have a brand-new life, reducing the strain that discarded leather can cause on landfills around the world.

▶ ## CARE ADVICE

Because Panama Trimmings labels are so durable, they do not require any special care. Zen advises that they are washed at home and that high temperatures be avoided in both the washing and drying cycles.

# LINEN

Did you know that the world's oldest textile is also one of its most sustainable — and that it's uniquely produced in our own backyard? Humankind has been using linen since 36,000 B.C., taking advantage of its versatility and durability. Evidence shows that it has been evolving with us, as our ancestors played with dyes and used it in ways that would greatly shape our relationship with the material, even today.

The fresh, light, supple fabric, made from flax fibres grown by dedicated European farmers, has undergone incredible innovation in recent years. New knitting techniques and textile blends have opened the door to endless possibilities for linen, from traditional breezy summer shirts and cozy winter sweaters to sporting equipment, stereo speakers, car components, and furniture.

Linen's versatility is complemented by its sustainable characteristics. Flax requires no irrigation, is GMO- and defoliant-free, and the flax fields capture 250,000 tons of carbon dioxide emissions, making it a carbon sink that provides significant benefits to the environment, especially when compared to cotton. During production, all parts of the flax stalk are used, generating zero material waste. Flax agriculture and production require no water, while the finishing stages require similar amounts to other cellulosic fibres that helps save nearly 20 litres every day someone wears a linen shirt.

The environmental impact of linen can be measured by its Higg MSI impact index, which is 95; in comparison, cotton's impact is 98. The Higg index was developed to provide a standardized way of comparing the ecological impact of the most popular textiles worldwide, and is used by brands, consumers, and producers to obtain a better understanding of products. Marie Demaegdt, textile and sustainability manager of the CELC, adds that linen's Higg index was currently under revision based on recent studies.

Europe alone is responsible for producing 85 percent of the world's flax fibre supply, as the region's unique combination of soil, climate, humidity, and generations of know-how create the perfect conditions for flaxseed to grow. "These three components make the success of linen in Europe", explains Alain Camilleri, communication director of the European Confederation of Flax and Hemp (CELC). "We knew that some other countries wanted to produce linen, but they don't have the same alchemy and the same ingredients". Above all else, flax is a fibre of proximity. It doesn't need to travel far to reach the end consumer — which is not only great for the environment, but also highly convenient for the European market. Flax fields extend throughout the continent, spanning the coasts of northern France, Belgium, and the Netherlands — the top flax producers. Linen production techniques have been passed down from generation to generation, possibly dating all the way back to 36,000 B.C. with the dyed linen fibre that archaeologists discovered in a Georgian cave. This ancient fibre proves that there is a special relationship between ancient human settlements and modern society.

## PRODUCTION JOURNEY

Before linen finds a home in consumer closets, it undergoes a transformative journey, starting as a little seed, planted and sown in March and April, when the fresh spring rains act as its only irrigation system. In June, the green stalks reach their full height, finishing their growth cycle by blooming a purple-blue flower. The stalks are then pulled up by special machines that preserve their full length, bundled, and left in the sun from July to September. Rainwater, morning dew, and rays of sunshine work their magic to loosen the flax fibres from the hard inner core of the stalk. The fibres are extracted, then hackled, or combed, and combined with other batches of fibres to form long, soft ribbons. The ribbons are twisted to form yarn using various techniques that create different types of yarn - thin and fine yarns for use in clothes and houseware, or thick and rough ones for home furnishings and rope. Skilled craftsmen transform the yarn into the final material, either by weaving or knitting the strands together. As an incredibly versatile fabric, linen can be finished and decorated in various ways — it can be dyed any colour, patterned, or printed, and recent innovations now allow for flame retardancy and water resistance. In the past, these finishings have been linen's weak link in the battle for sustainability, as they are usually high-impact procedures, but new developments in eco-friendly, water-repellent solutions and natural dye stuffs have improved these processes. "Flax farmers are very often people who were keen to be sustainable from the beginning", Demaegdt tells us. "That's why we are so sustainable now. They are really always interested in doing better". For the last three years, the CELC has launched awareness campaigns all over Europe called "I Love Linen" to inform consumers and fashion brands about all of the exciting innovations in the linen industry. The campaign also intends to modernize the perception of linen, and to help consumers understand this material and what they are investing in. Camilleri explains that "buying linen is buying an eco-responsible fibre, but also a fibre of history". In the United Kingdom, for instance, linen has been traditionally used more for home wear than for fashion, and the campaign,

Photo: Christoph Kobler / Vieböck

implemented in the country in 2018, sought to highlight the fabric's use in all U.K. markets, and especially among fashion brands. The CELC formed a special collaboration with John Lewis and around 300 British boutiques, highlighting the benefits of linen and its multiple uses in the fashion industry. At the end of the campaign, Lewis reported a 175 percent increase in the demand for linen. "When you open minds to the different characteristics of linen, you can convince your consumer and the public", Camilleri continues.

## THE ROLE OF INNOVATION

Demagdt remembers linen nearly disappearing from the fashion industry over the past 30 or 40 years, but under the influence of passionate designers, who understood the real value of the fabric and were introducing linen to their collections, it gradually returned to the market. Everything has changed since then. These last 10 years have seen a flurry of developments that have completely revolutionized our perception about linen and its uses, the most significant of which have been the introduction of washed linen and knitted linen.

No longer do you have to worry about excessive creasing with your linen products — with a washed linen finish, the resulting fabric is soft, smooth, and doesn't need to be ironed. These traits are useful around the home, especially for bed and table linens, stylish garments, and accessories. Knitted linens use a circular knitting technique that is standard for making jerseys, like polo shirts and sweatshirts. The technique has gained popularity because it leaves this natural material with a crease-resistant, elastic bounce that differs drastically from the woven options most people have become accustomed to. Before, it was impossible to use linen yarns in the knitting process, since it was done on rapid machines using very fine needles, which led to either yarn or needle breakage. Now, knitting allows for the production of regular, fine, yet strong yarns that provide an attractive option for the apparel market, Demaegdt explains. With this type of knitting, linen is not produced using the orthogonal, or perpendicular, yarn crossing, but instead is formed with loops that are naturally crease-resistant and elastic. "So, the construction of knitting is a very good complement to the linen yarn, because the linen yarn is not elastic", Demaegdt adds.

As a result, knitted jersey-type apparel currently comprises about 25 percent of linen sales and woven material comprises the other 75 percent. Ten years ago, the market for apparel was 100 percent woven, reflecting the changes the market is undergoing.

## VALUE OF THE FABRIC

The CELC identifies 15 characteristics that make linen a worthwhile fabric and investment: ecological, zero waste, biodegradability, breathability, thermoregulation, absorbency, colour-taking capability, resistency, stiffness and lightness, thermal and sound insulation, vibration absorption, hypoallergenic and anti-bacterial properties, proximity and traceability, and it even promotes relaxation and sleep. For Demaegdt, it's the combination of all 15 characteristics that makes linen a "noble material" that can be used in a myriad of ways. The fabric is ready for any stylistic direction, from a more baroque to a more craft look. In any case, there are plenty of possibilities to integrate linen into any collection, from ready-to-wear to sportswear to leisure, and from bed linens to bath and spa accessories.

Linen's uniqueness is validated by a comfort performance study conducted by the CELC, which compared it to other commonly used fabrics, like cotton, viscose, and polyester. One hundred percent linen fabrics consistently outperformed the rest in many of the categories examined, and scored the highest comfort index. Linen performs the best for ventilation, contributing to a cooling effect important for sports activities; breathability, which is the flow of moisture vapor through the fabric; and absorption and moisture management, which is the removal of moisture from the body to the outer surface of the fabric. It also performs second best in terms of heat insulation, after polyester. These qualities make linen a sublime material for making comfortable, breathable clothes that find a compromise between coolness and heat retention.

In other words, flax fibre is a natural performance fibre that can easily be associated with its technical synthetic counterparts. Designers can take advantage of these characteristics when developing sports and athleisure wear — the material's breathability and thermoregulating characteristics can be blended with water-repellent solutions to create the ultimate fabric for chic, comfortable city wear that adapts to the modern-day active lifestyle. These styles reflect the "cross-fertilization" that's been seen between active sportswear trends and the more traditional, formal, clean-cut style – a crossover that springs from people's desire to wear the same garment for different occasions throughout the day. People want clothes you can, for example, wear to work and ride a bike home in afterwards. "Performance will be more important for our lifestyle and [will] spread across various stylistic directions", Demaegdt says. She sees these novelties entering the sportswear and athleisure markets slowly, item by item: in knitted fleece sweatshirts, or in Lacoste's new polo made from an equal blend of cotton and linen from their SS19 collection.

Linen is an amazing, sustainable textile — with a price point to match. Its rarity and labour-intensive process raise the cost of linen products, especially in comparison to materials like cotton. Currently, it comprises less than 1 percent of the world's fibre market, and some people may be put off by the seemingly steep price point, Demaegdt admits. But, she continues, "linen doesn't want to become the new cotton or replace other fibres", it wants to remain a niche, quality market, comparable to that of cashmere and other luxury materials, but at a lower price. With its positive qualities, the fabric sells itself — it doesn't require extravagant marketing or storytelling techniques, Camilleri says. "We just have to talk about the true qualities of linen: to say the truth and talk about its history", he says. Consumers can further ensure that they are buying the best quality European linen by looking for the Masters of Linen certification and the European Flax guarantee, both of which verify traceability of the fabric — the former as a guarantee of fibre origin, and the latter of fibre processing conducted completely in Europe. Global linen markets are gradually growing, especially in India and China, as the fabric's characteristics become better known. These Asian markets are transforming the biggest volumes of the European fibre, providing numerous and affordable linen options, while Europe produces smaller volumes with high levels of excellency. To experts, this suggests that consumption patterns in these large economies are slowly changing, since it was once thought that consumers were more influenced by trends and brands rather

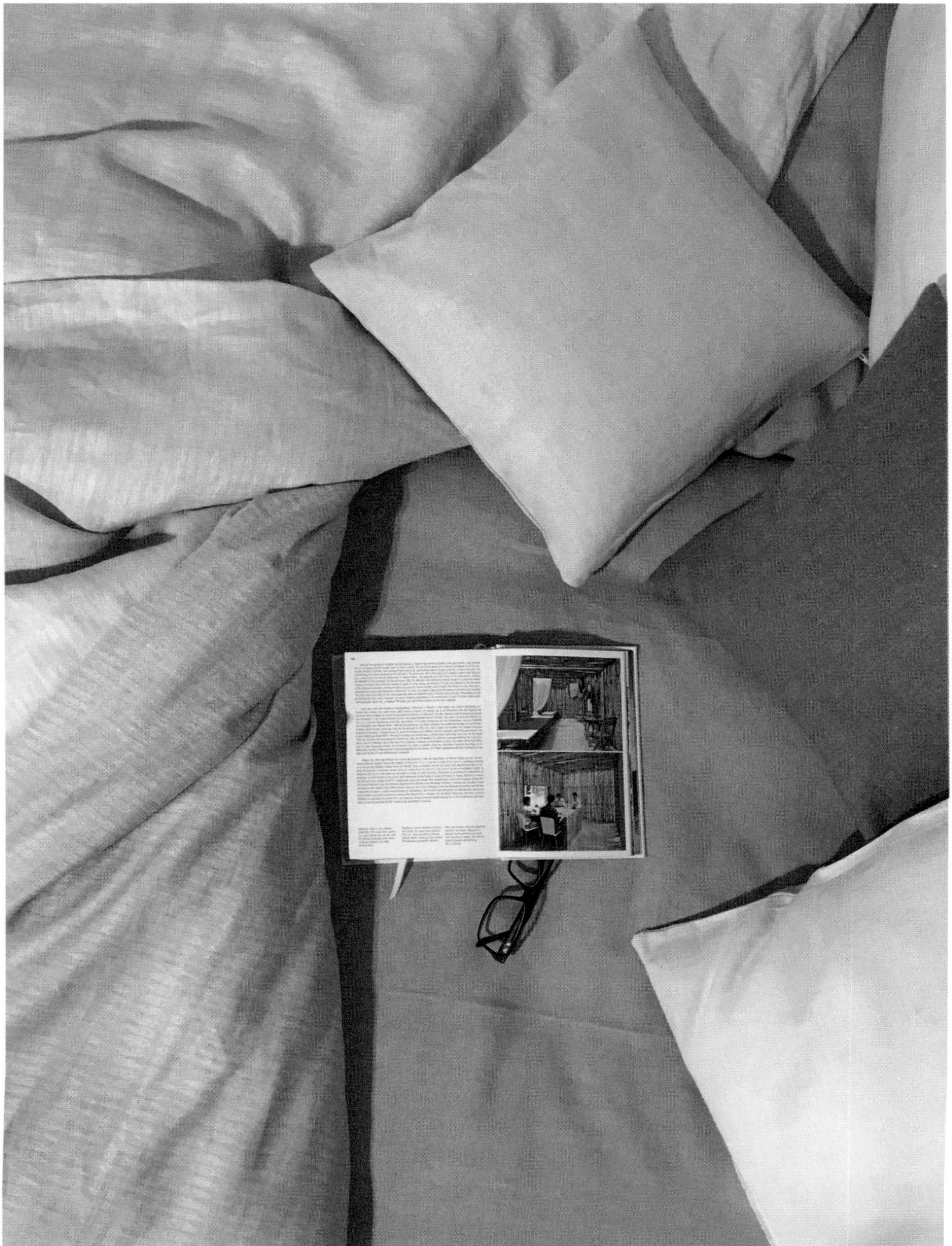

than materials, Demaegdt reflects. Hopefully the change is a positive indicator of an ongoing movement towards sustainability around the world, she says. Regardless, in her opinion, sustainability is not enough to drive a designer to use linen in their designs or enough to persuade a consumer to buy a garment; the material also needs to be innovative and creative, which linen certainly is. Instead, Demaegdt believes sustainability should be a basic element of any garment, and all other performance values are a bonus.

▶ **CARE ADVICE**

People still have the wrong perception that linen is difficult to care for, but with today's developments, that couldn't be further from the truth. Most linens can be hand- or machine- washed, but they must be washed with a lot of water to make them last longer. Otherwise, the natural fibres can become chafed and destroyed, explains Christoph Kobler, an Austrian linen manufacturer from Vieböck. If using a washing machine, linens should be soaked in water for a while beforehand to ensure the fibre's integrity. Some — not all! — can even be tumble-dried on low, depending on the manufacturer's instructions, but in general, you should avoid machine drying linen as it can also damage the fibre, Kobler adds. Unlike cotton, it doesn't become threadbare with each wash — in fact, it forms a lovely patina and gets more durable as time goes on. Today's linens no longer require people to slave over the ironing board, as most products dry with minimal creasing. To ensure that garments do not get too crushed, experts recommend ironing while the fabric is still damp with a medium-hot setting. Storing linens could not be easier, as all they need is a cool, dry place — preferably not in plastic bags, cardboard boxes or cedar chests. To avoid creasing, hang your linen clothes on wooden hangers.

## Q&A WITH CHRISTOPH KOBLER, AUSTRIAN LINEN MANUFACTURER FROM VIEBÖCK

**Q:** *Can you please explain the process and production? What is the path for the sustainable manufacturing of linen fabrics at Vieböck?*

**A:** In order to get a high-quality linen fabric you have to start with the purchase of the yarns. We only use linen yarns (GOTS and conventional) from Europe. The spinning process of the flax fibre is done in Italy and Latvia. If we decide to use coloured linen yarn, we send the material to a German dyeing [company]. After the delivery of the linen yarns we start the production in our weaving mill in Helfenberg (Austria). Five weavers ensure that every single fabric [is of] perfect quality. Afterwards, the raw fabrics will be sent to a finisher. The finishing company is about 90 kilometres away from our weaving mill. After the finishing-process (washing, calendaring, and dyeing) we deliver Vieböck linen to the whole world.

**Q:** *What qualities and performance characteristics makes these fibres unique from a quality point of view?*

**A:** Many people think that linen is a hard, rough, and uncomfortable material, however, it depends very much on the finishing process. If you use suitable finishing methods, you can offer linen fabrics [that] are smooth, soft, thin, and light.

**Q:** *What role does innovation play in producing your linen?*

**A:** We create remarkable new fibre blends to make new designs and fabrics. For instance: linen and hemp, linen and wool, or linen with viscose.

**Q:** *How do customers view linen today?*

**A:** Nowadays, people accept and love the characteristics of this wonderful, natural product. Moreover, our customers really want to know where the fabrics and the flax come from. It is very important to offer a regional, sustainable, and natural product.

**Q:** *What are the drawbacks of using these fabrics? Cost? Performance?*

**A:** Actually, [the] demand for linen is very high, and as a consequence, the price of linen yarn is increasing more and more. We have to deal with the high purchasing price and the insufficient availability of the raw materials.

**Q:** *Finally, what future do you see for linen and for the sustainable fashion movement in Europe in general?*

**A:** In my opinion, sustainable fashion is the only way we should go, and can go. We have to encourage our customers to buy less and buy fair, high-quality products. If we are able to convince the customers, we are also able to save our resources. Linen and the [...] flax plant are very helpful for sustainable fashion because flax needs little water and no fertilizer!!

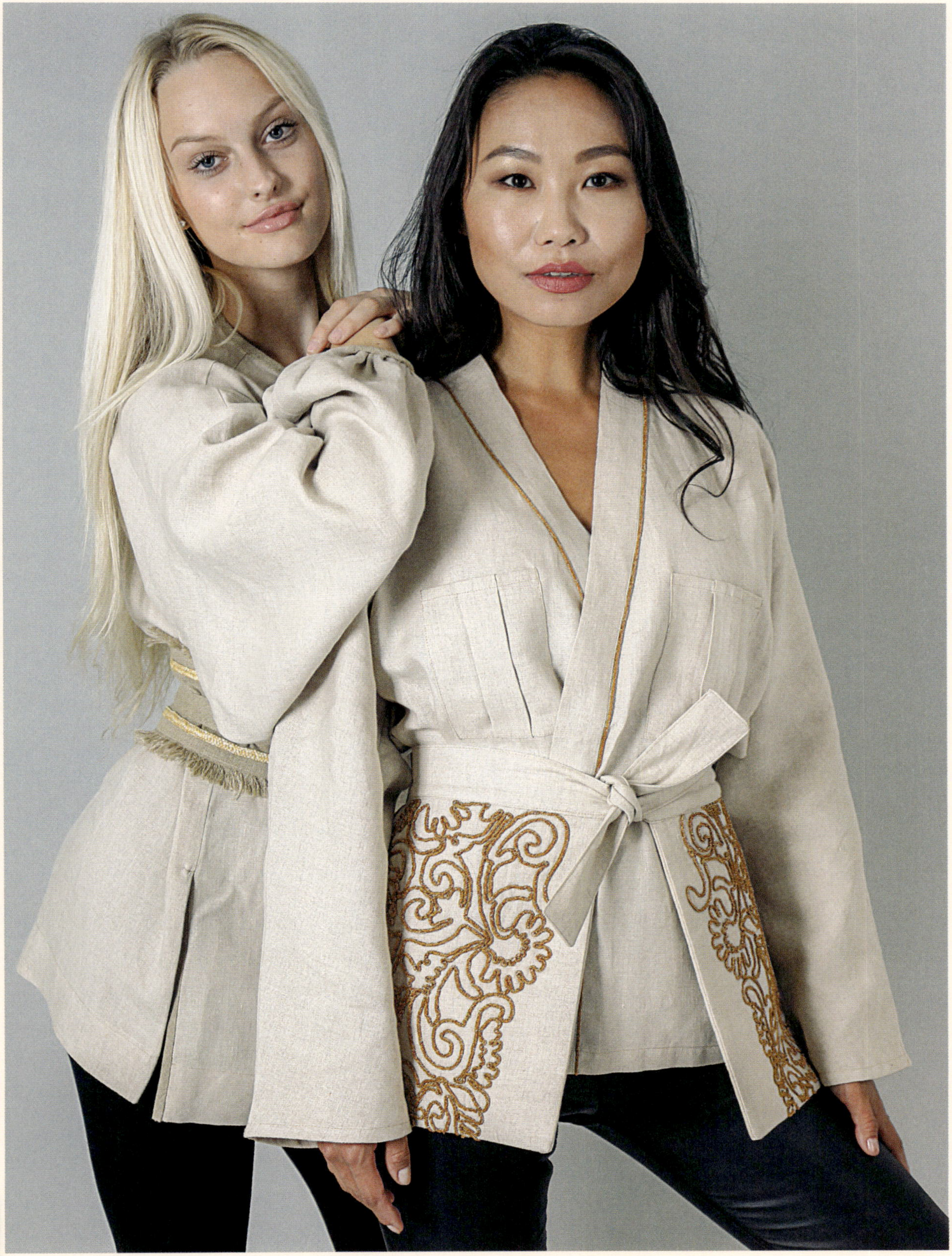

# WOOL

Wool has been used to dress the world since humanity was born; it has also been innovated and recycled. Nowadays, this natural fibre can benefit the planet and serve consumer needs with less impact than many man-made fibres. The downside, though, is that the price and the labour-intensive production process of wool predetermine its position in the fibre market. As a consequence, wool remains in a niche sector, accounting for 1.1 percent of all global fibre consumption. Another element affecting its production, consumption, and price is climate change. The entire wool production cycle is adversely affected due to the increase in temperature, with consequences on land exploitation and animal breeding, which ultimately affect the quantity and quality of the fibre.

Alberto Rossi, Business Development Manager at Chargeurs, a company with a long history of working with farmers and selling wool since the 19th century, describes the situation from an insider perspective. Within the last fifteen years, most producers have decreased wool production in favour of other agricultural commodities to have a better return. Because of all the changes within the fibre market, in addition to environment-related changes, the production cost for wool growers is increasing and so their income is decreasing.

According to the International Wool Textile Organisation (IWTO), on a global scale, 300 million families from rural areas are dependent on sheep and goat farming to survive. The decrease in wool production has been significant in several geographic areas; wool production has decreased by 20 percent in China, 19 percent in Australia, 11 percent in CIS, 7 percent in New Zealand, and 2 percent in Argentina, South Africa, and the United Kingdom. The wool sector needs scientific and technological contributions to support farmers with practical and efficient solutions and usher in an era of positive change with solutions to economic and environmental problems.

## PRODUCTION JOURNEY

By definition, wool is natural and sustainable. It grows on sheep, and once a year, the sheep are shorn to avoid health risks like overheating, discomfort, and disease. Wool farmers take care to avoid possible land desertification by constantly shifting their animals to different pastures. The only requirements for raising healthy sheep are water, grass, sun, and air, with no need for chemical or synthetic products. Geographical areas and their climates determine the number of sheep that can be reared per hectare. "In Patagonia, it's one sheep per hectare. In Australia, it is 10 sheep per hectare because there's much more [grass]", Rossi explains. In fact, wool farmers have only one asset – the land on which to feed and raise their animals. It's in their best interest to keep the land in good shape, with no desertification or pollution. The mental and physical condition of the sheep is another responsibility faced by farmers who want to succeed in the wool farming business. Chargeurs controls these factors by certifying that every farmer in its network complies with a set of rules for animal welfare and land management prescribed by Charguer's NATIVA protocol, which assures those values are honoured from farm to store. The common practice known as mulesing – the surgical way to shear wool – is banned by the protocol. Farmers' compliance with the rules is verified by third-party auditing companies, such as ICEA in Italy, annual Control Union or NSF certifications and random visits to the farms, Rossi adds. Chargeurs has certified 500 wool farmers across the world in Uruguay, Argentina, South Africa, Australia, and Tasmania. After shearing, a company scours the wool to produce wool tops; then these raw materials are sold to yarn manufacturers. At a later stage, the yarn is spun, then transformed into different products and blended with different ingredients, based on a brand's needs.

## VALUE OF THE FABRIC

Wool is like a grape, says Rossi: "You can put the grape into [a] different part of the world, but the result will not be the same. "High-quality wool usually comes from regions with rich grasslands generated by the right amount of rainfall. Slightly finer wool is produced in arid places like Patagonia, where there is less grass. The breed of sheep is another factor that influences the quality of wool. Coarse wool comes from South America due to the prevalence of crossbred sheep. Merino wool, on the other hand, originates from Australia. Even if the length and diameter of a fibre is the same, the fibre's origin also affects its feel. So wool from Uruguay has a different feel compared to wool from Tasmania. Every product needs a different type of wool, and it's impossible to say where the finest wool originates. Rossi suggests designers first determine the purpose of their final product, and then get back to finding the best wool to realize the characteristics of what they want to make. South American wool would be more appropriate for car or aircraft seats, due to the strong and sound characteristics of the fibre. With 27, 28, or 30 microns, the seats will be durable and resistant.

Wool is a miraculous fibre, and it's given to us by nature. Humans have never been able to replicate the assets and performance of wool fibre, and it's not comparable to any other fabric. Wool is naturally odour-resistant, fire-resistant, thermoregulating, elastic, air pollution-absorbent, renewable, and fully biodegradable. It's also the best performing fibre in the world. When wool is worn next to the skin in products like socks, underwear, and base layers of active sportswear, it naturally thermoregulates body temperature, keeping us warm in the winter and cool and dry in the summer. For this reason, people wear wool even in desert areas, Rossi states. Diving into market segments and product applications, wool can be found everywhere, from high-end brands to the commercial market. For luxury menswear products, like jackets, high-end brands blend wool with silk or cashmere to enhance every single characteristic of this precious fibre. If men's suits are often made with pure wool at the higher end of the market, more affordable products have a blended composition, such as wool with acrylic, etc. For sweaters, high-end brands typically use pure wool, and sweaters made with a wool/ acrylic blend are usually found in the lower price range. Active sportswear demands wool for its performance in the base layers of garments made for running, hiking, or skiing. The wool used in these garments is mainly blended with other fibres. Only a niche segment in active sportswear can afford to offer pure wool. In the technical segment, like the automotive industry, wool is always present and blended with other fibres.

## SUSTAINABILITY + TRACEABILITY

There is no difference between sustainable and conventional wool, either in terms of quality, or technical specifications, like micron length or quantity. However, sustainable wool offers full transparency and control in sourcing and production, reassuring customers by giving information about where the wool was sourced, how the animals were treated, which wool farmer raised the animals, and how the mill processed the fibre. In conventional wool sourcing, none of these factors are present. "You just buy a black box", Rossi states. Conventional wool is often offered as a blend of wool with different origins and qualities. Fine and inferior fibres are blended to achieve a price point that will satisfy a customer's budget. In the case of traceable, sustainable, and certified wool, companies have to disclose the original source of the fibre, Rossi explains. Chargeurs is one of the first companies in the textile industry to adopt blockchain technology to certify the traceability of its wool along the supply chain, from farm to retail. Blockchain technology provides a new level of traceability in a digital format, where the data is uploaded by all participants involved in the production process. Once two parties upload the data and validate each other, no one can modify or manipulate the data. Then, the transaction certificate, which authenticates the entire chain of custody, is uploaded into the blockchain, which again proves the previous steps were correctly managed. For example, company A sent 3 kilos of yarn to company B. In this case, the recipient of the raw materials has to communicate the outcome and the realized product. The audit company can check the data too, but once it's uploaded in blockchain, the data can't be changed or worded differently, Rossi adds. Through the QR code generated by blockchain and printed on garment labels, end customers can see all the steps involved in the realization of a product. Rossi explains that other available methods to trace fabrics are done on paper, which can be easily modified or manipulated. He explains how the system works: "the spinning mill can buy only 10 kilos of certified wool, and with that, they can produce 50 kilos of certified yarn". They show the same certificate to five different customers, and nobody is able to cross-check the data of what was actually in the yarn that they received. Nowadays, blockchain is the most trusted solution in the textile industry which can prove best practice for fibre sourcing to all consumers. In addition, everything has its price: a sustainable package with traceable credentials, and even product marketing, would raise the final price point by 15 percent, as compared to the price of conventional wool per kilo. But the price of a final product will cost 3 euros more, which seems affordable, Rossi concludes.

▶ **CARE ADVICE**

Wool garments can last up to 20 or 30 years, if treated properly. The fibre has a few particularities as well, namely moths and shrinkage. Only store clean wool items and protect them from insects when changing garments between seasons. Always check the care label on a garment before deciding whether to hand wash or machine wash your wool items. Wash each item briefly at a low temperature and on a delicate wool cycle to avoid strong mechanical actions, otherwise the garment might shrink. Wool can be self-cleaned in a more natural way by leaving the garment outside in fresh air on a foggy day. The day after, it should be ready to wear. Its natural composition allows wool to be washed less than any other fibre, saving energy and water.

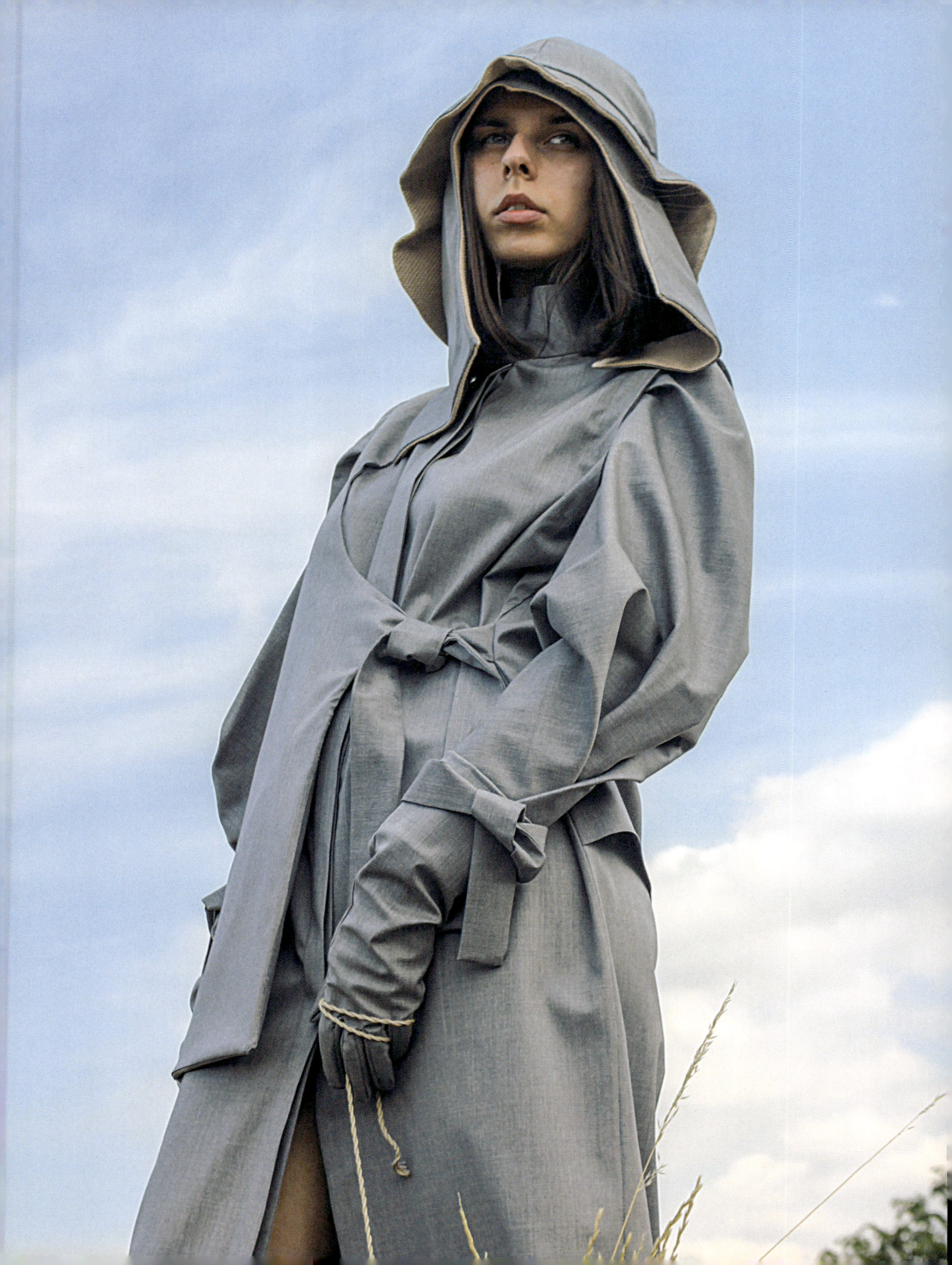

# SILK

A beautiful natural product such as silk has long been cultivated on silk farms run by family businesses across the globe. India is the second world producer of silk after China, a country that, in recent years, went through a huge economic transformation, from poverty to wealth, although profit for many local silk farmers remains under question. So how can silk change lives? This was the question that fashion designer Chandra Prakash Jha had in his mind, before knowing that peace silk would become his lifelong journey. He carried out extensive research evaluating the ecological, financial, and social aspects of this peculiar production. It was during a visit to a silk farm that he realized he could leave a mark and help to improve the livelihood of local citizens from his native country. After six months of experimentation, he realized a nonviolent peace silk fabric, made respecting the ecosystem and without killing the silkworm. That's how Cocccon was born in 2011. When he first showed his creation at Green Showroom in Germany, he remembers how "a lot of people didn't know how silk was made". After a while, things started to change, and Cocccon spread through a community of people sharing an interest in the ethical side of fashion, and it has been a real breakthrough to cultivate awareness of this sustainable luxury fabric.

In 2016, Cocccon was established as a separate entity apart from the Jha designer brand, focusing on the production of silk fabrics contributing to the development of sustainable fashion towards being glamorous and dazzling.

## PRODUCTION JOURNEY

The production of silk begins with sericulture, as a foundation to cultivate, and rear silkworms. Although the process occurs naturally, its management determines the quality of the silk. The raw material is made by nature and spun in the form of cocoons by silkworms, which today are fully domesticated by silk farmers, reared either indoors or in a wild environment. Silkworms are divided into races based on geographical distribution: Japanese, Chinese, Tropical, European, and Korean, and the quality of the silk thread is highly affected by ambient temperature, rearing seasons, and food base, all resulting in different end products.

Among the many factors influencing the success of sericulture is also the environment, specifically pollution issues, due to the overuse of chemicals, fertilizers and pesticides, an obstacle to the sustainable development of local agriculture and its products. In 2012, a conventional Indian based silk farm in Jiharkand was taken over by Cocccon to re-establish the entire silk cultivation-weaving process. During experiments, Jha found that 90 percent of the chemicals commonly used were completely unnecessary. From the outset, it was important that no chemicals were used in Cocccon's cultivation process. This ensures that the sericulture is organic and the host plants, the Mulberry trees, are producing quality food – their leaves – to feed silkworms. Wild silk – as it is also known – is a rare product, produced in wild conditions, which means the silkworms have to be protected from predators. Cocccon keeps insects and birds away simply by covering the host tree with a mosquito net. In the tropical conditions of India, the Mulberry tree root disease is another common issue mostly prevented by treating trees with chemicals. Instead of applying harmful substances, Jha uses a liquid spray made of plant extracts with medicinal properties to solve the issue without any toxic side effects for the ecosystem. The ethical aspect of Cocccon's peace silk production respects not only the environment but also silkworms. Three days to a maximum of one week is the usual lifespan of these little insects, and it might sound trivial, but it's more than an ephemeral life according to Cocccon, whose philosophy is rooted in Indian spiritual beliefs where everything has the right to life. To ensure the natural cycle is not interrupted, Cocccon avoids the use of boiled water to cook the pupae alive inside of their cocoon. Jha makes it clear, "One peace silk scarf saves almost a thousand lives". Instead of following the traditional silk process, Cocccon makes a small hole in the cocoon when the moth is ready to fly away, keeping the precious casing, from which a short-stapled fibre is created.

On the one hand, technological innovation helped in developing and almost reinventing Cocccon's silk production process, but Jha is still looking for the right solution to produce superior quality silk with a high aesthetic appeal. The first non-violent silk products reaching the fashion market had some quality drawbacks. Jha admits, "Initially many people didn't like our silk because it had a lot of flaws and holes", but now the quality is getting better, he explains, adding that in a couple of years, peace silk would reach the same quality standard as conventional silk. Once the filament is obtained from the cocoon, the fibre is cleaned in hot water with bio-soup to eliminate natural impurities and maintain its typical cream or beige colour. The white colour traditionally associated with silk is, in reality, a combination of two elements: the indoor cultivation of silkworms and a purifying process that requires a chemical based bleaching agent. Naturally, the colour of the native fibre may have different shades depending on the cultivation methods, seasonality and silkworm race. To make the colour uniform, Cocccon uses the most preferable method, namely Hydrogen Peroxide.

Coccoon's entire production process is certified, from the cultivation of silkworms to the creation of silk fabrics and their printing. Willing to guarantee his brand's transparency about organic production and fair compensation to his workers, Jha sought a GOTS certification to stress their focus on social and ecological factors. This decision has made Coccoon more attractive to potential clients, due in part to the certification's credibility, but also to the possibility of visiting the silk farm to have a close-up look at the peace silk production.

## **VALUE OF THE FABRIC**

For centuries people have known the value of shiny, soft silk, which has always been considered a luxurious material, ideal for making beautiful dresses to wear during key events and important occasions, like official ceremonies or to highlight a noble status. The properties of this natural fibre also make silk garments durable, comfortable, and easy to wear, other reasons for its success. Despite its loss of popularity, silk still occupies a luxury niche, while other fabrics offered themselves for more functional uses. The biggest advantage of non-violent silk lies in its being good for the ecosystem, as well

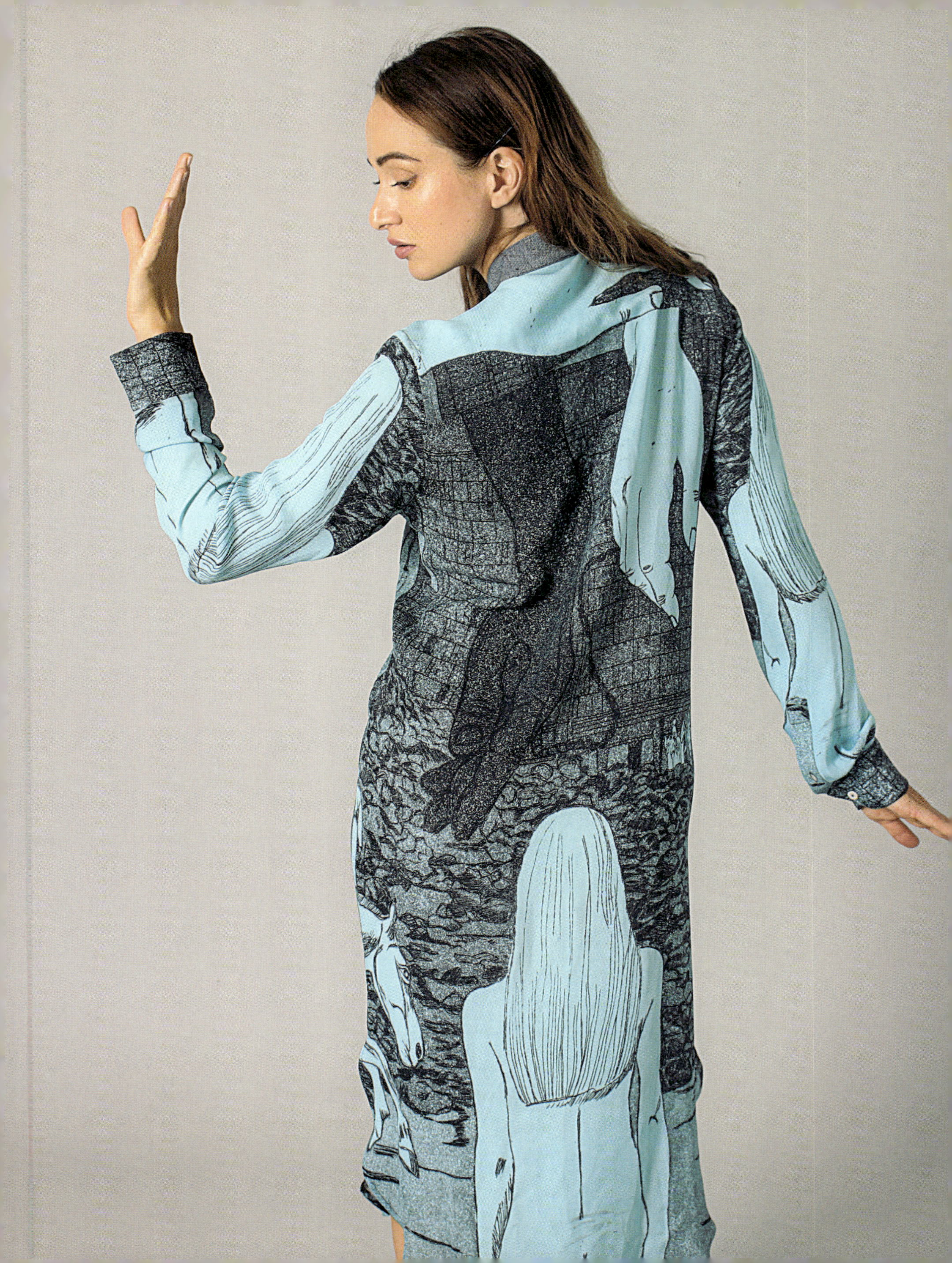

as customer health, since an investment in sustainable products would pay off in the long term. The price point is the biggest question for many fibres, especially silk. Jha himself admits that peace silk fabrics are more expensive than, for instance, the Chinese counter offer. Chinese silk, in particular, operates within China's price dumping policy that exports products at below production cost. This strategy has accustomed overseas markets like Europe and America to have access to silk at lower prices. This price competition consequently reduced the local production market, lowering profit rates.

Coccoon's prices are 40 to 60 percent more expensive than Eastern silk and 20 to 25 percent more expensive than the normal value of European silk. Nevertheless, Cocccon has reached a powerful spread across the world, primarily developing business relations with start-ups and individual designers who see value in non-violent organic silk production. Jiha confirms that India remains a leading market for the consumption of sustainable products, and unlike in other countries, there is no mass shopping culture as people continue to shop primarily in boutiques, thus contributing to sustainable fashion's development.

▶ **CARE ADVICE**

Cocccon peace silk has the same properties as regular silk. Washing silk at home, with cold water is recommended by the company, unless the label says DRY-CLEAN only. Jiha recommends avoiding the use of specialized chemical products to clean silk and instead suggests a delicate care recipe, commonly used in India. Add baby shampoo or natural-based Indian washing nuts in cold-water to wash silk garments by hands. Washing nuts should be left in the water overnight. They will dissolve in the liquid by morning. Silk can be ironed too, but at a lower temperature. If you don't know how to iron it, ask an expert on silk.

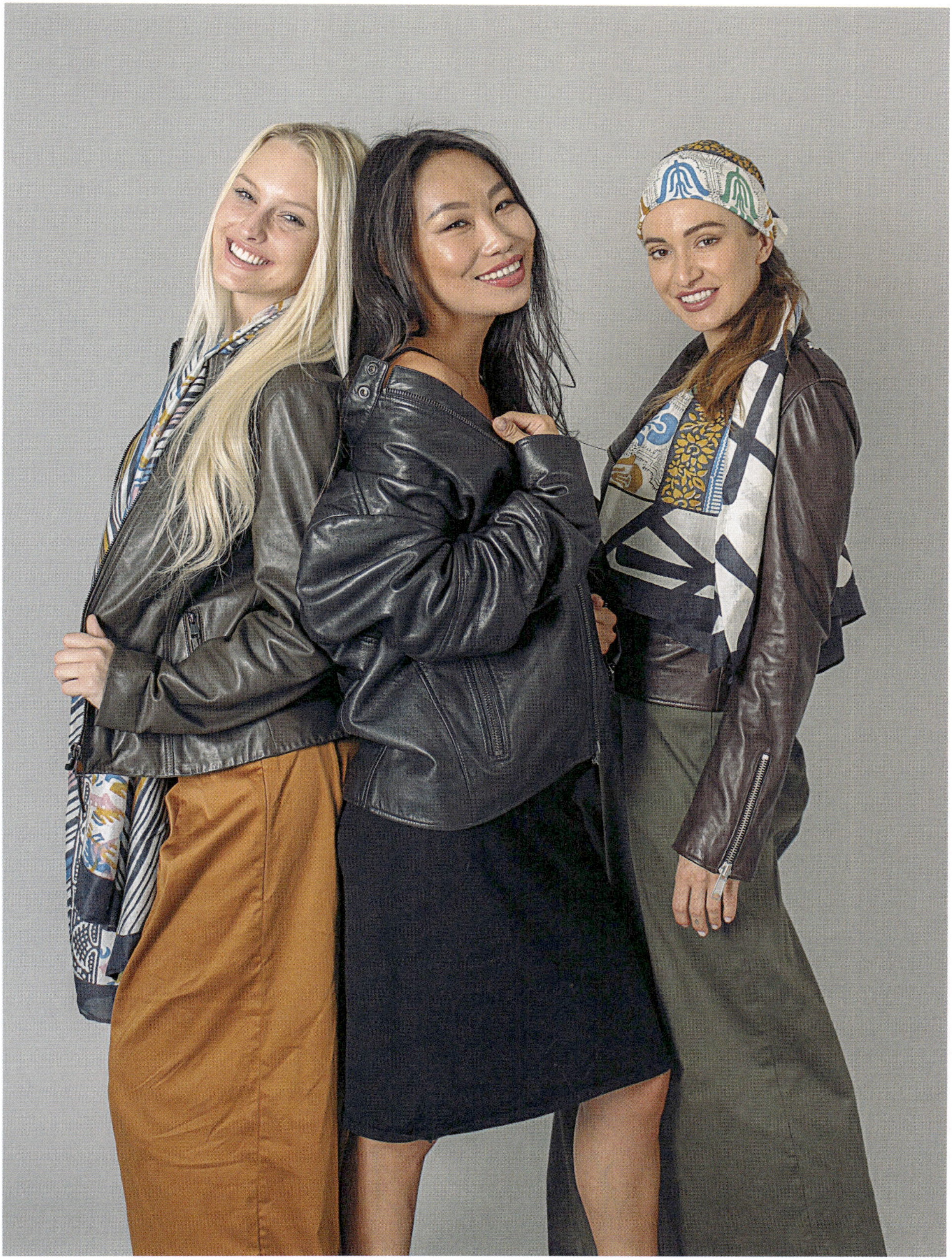

# ALTERNATIVES TO LEATHER

No textile appeals to the senses as much as leather does. Everything, from its smell to its smooth-to-the-touch finish and its rich, vivid hues, conveys the ultimate sense of luxury, class and finesse. Leather products play an important part in the world economy, with a global trade value of about US $100 billion per year — an amount that is only increasing in response to a growing global population, according to a United Nations report. As the demand for leather products — such as bags, shoes, clothes, saddlery and car and furniture upholstery — increases, so do the environmental strains caused by the leather industry. Around 80 to 90 percent of manufacturers use a chromium-based chemical process called tanning to transform raw animal hides into consumer-ready leather. The effects of using chromium salts can range from contaminating water sources and affecting soil acidity levels to causing detrimental health effects for the workers tanning the hides.

Archaeological evidence shows that ancient civilizations, including the Romans and Egyptians, used bark, root and berry extracts to make their leather products more resistant to decay. Today, those same methods are used in vegetable-based tanning processes, which some manufacturers use as an alternative to the more polluting option of heavy metal chromium. But conventional vegetable tanning methods are costly and less popular, as it can take up to two months to tan leather via this process. The resulting material tends to be heavier and stiffer than its chrome-tanned counterpart and lacks chrome-tanned leather's colour versatility and water-resistance.

## OLIVE LEATHER

Everybody loves olive oil for its ability to spice up even the simplest of dishes. What few people know is that the olive plant has a secret: an ingredient that has the potential to reduce the environmental impact of leather production and tanning. A team of German researchers, located within the walls of the former German Leather Institute, discovered the ingredient while experimenting with the biotechnology of leather during their pursuit to find a sustainable alternative to chrome and chrome-free tanning chemicals. These enthusiasts found a "magic molecule", called olive oleuropein, in the leaves of the olive tree. This bitter-tasting molecule allowed the production of incredibly soft vegetable-tanned leather for the very first time – leather which can be used to make a wide variety of products.

There seem to be no limits to what olive-tanned leather, patented as Olivenleder®, can achieve, from apparel, bags, accessories, and footwear to more delicate, refined products, such as luxury car upholstery and gloves – "which in the past was never possible", says Thomas Lamparter, head of sales at wet-green GmbH. Wet-green GmbH is the German company that spearheaded the research into non-toxic tanning and created a real opportunity for the leather industry to be less harmful to the environment by patenting the Olivenleder® tanning agent. This agent won the "healthy tanning agent" title in a Cradle to Cradle certification assessment due to its numerous benefits. The assessment takes multiple criteria into account, including sustainability, environmental impact, product durability, and social and health benefits — and Olivenleder passed with flying colours. The Olivenleder solution places no limits on order volumes, making it accessible for brands who need everything from very small volumes to large, industrial sized quantities. It opens the door for every sort of business to implement this solution, from individual designers to small and medium enterprises to major brands. Brands that "might want to move away from leather, but actually like leather" will likely be the first ones to substitute Olivenleder for the conventional material in their designs, Lamparter believes.

## LEATHER

When we, as customers, step into the leather market, we can opt to either purchase products made with natural leather or with alternative, man-made materials, like faux or vegan leather. In order to make an informed decision about our investment, we need to have a clear idea of the characteristics of those materials, like their usage, longevity, colour, and texture, and then consider the price point.

Most vegan leathers are produced with synthetic materials such as PVC and PU — non-biodegradable petroleum products that release polluting microplastics into the environment. Critics of vegan leather emphasize that its durability is inferior to that of genuine leather, contributing to consumer waste in a way that traditional leather does not. Thus, genuine leather can be more environmentally friendly than its vegan counterpart. Nevertheless, faux leather has a trick up its sleeve that can make it a more attractive offer: a lower price point, which drives the decision-making process for many. Global consumption trends suggest that 99.9 percent of leather production uses animal skins that are waste products from the meat and dairy industries.

"As long as people are eating meat or drinking milk, skins will be available and some[one] should use this material", Lamparter says. Although animal rights can become an issue when the hides are not ethically sourced, Olivenleder is only made of by-products from meat and dairy industries that employ ethical practices. "It's tanning a by-product — skin typically being a by-product from the meat or dairy industry — with a by-product", Lamparter explains.

## OLIVE LEAVES + SUSTAINABILITY

Before the "magic molecule" can transform animal hides into rich leather, it has to be transported from the breezy coasts of the Mediterranean to the tanning agent manufacturer in Germany. It then is either used by wet-green in Reutlingen, Germany, or supplied to partner tanneries around the world where it is used to manufacture Olivenleder for various industries. Olive oleuropein is a protein found in abundance in the skin, flesh, seeds, leaves and oil of the olive plant. It is the only plant protein used for tanning that is considered a cross-linker, meaning it can produce soft, pliable leather used

Photo: Olivenleder

in garments or saddlery; other vegetable tanning agents produce tougher, stiffer leathers often used for products like shoes. Because of its strong bitter taste, it must be completely removed from the fruit to make it edible. "It's not pleasant, but that bitter part is actually what our tanning agent [is]", Lamparter says. Olive leaves are a natural by-product of the olive oil industry and are sourced from the trees that cover the Mediterranean coast. Olivenleder's reliance on olive leaves, rather than on olive oil or the fruit itself, sets it apart from other vegetable tanning methods in terms of sustainability. Most conventional methods require separate harvests of the tanning agent — harvests that could produce food, or that require turning forest land into agricultural plots. The olive plant seems to be the only one that contains an agent that could be used for tanning leather.

Olivenleder uses the excess leaves that fall from the trees after the harvest — leaves that would otherwise be burnt. "So many leaves are available [that] you can already [...] replace 40 percent of global leather production, which is more than 700 million square metres of leather [today]", Lamparter says. Wet-green also uses freshly cut leaves from the branches of the olive tree, which are pruned every two years as part of a standard process done to ensure a constant olive harvest. The branches and leaves are then dried in the sun to conserve the oleuropein. Otherwise, the tanning agent — which is incredibly active in fresh leaves — would waste away by the time it arrives at the manufacturing plant.

The dried olive leaves then travel to Germany and are handed over to one of the largest manufacturers of herbal and fruit teas in the world. The olive-based tanning agent is extracted through a brewing process similar to tea-making in which the leaves are boiled in scalding hot water that is later evaporated to make a thick, bitter syrup. In the future, company executives hope to have a manufacturing centre closer to the Mediterranean which accounts for about 90 percent of global olive production, he says.

## TANNING TECHNIQUES

Once the syrup is extracted and shipped to partner tanneries all over the world, leather production begins. The tanning process used by Olivenleder

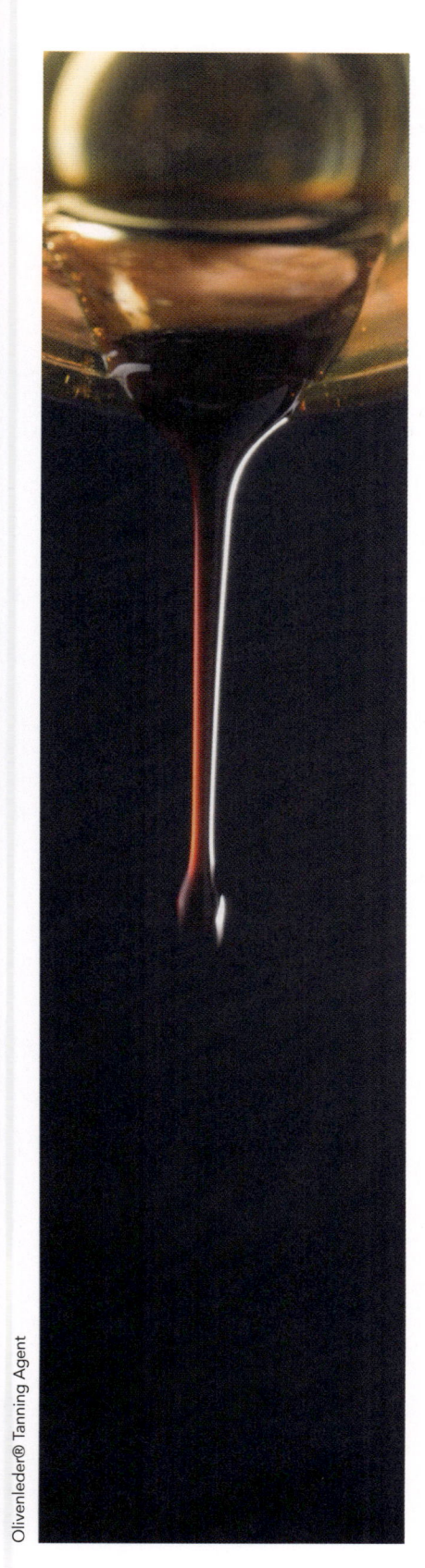

is, in essence, similar to that of conventional chrome-free tanning. The animal hides are soaked in drums with the tanning agent, creating the first line of leather that is then re-tanned and dyed. Unlike other vegetable tanning agents, which make a dark, richly-toned leather, the olive-based agent leaves the first line of material with a light beige colour — perfect for re-tanning and dyeing. Its light colour requires fewer dye products than chrome tanning agents and produces the same variety of bright colours. For a manufacturer to obtain an Olivenleder license, it needs to follow many quality standards throughout the tanning process and avoid cross-contamination with chrome and other hazardous, synthetic, chrome-free chemicals. Leathers can't be produced with dyes that contain heavy metals like nickel, cobalt or chromium, and instead must be dyed with acidic powdered dyes, similar to vinegar acetate, which are not harmful. These standards provide huge benefits to consumers, leather workers and designers. Olivenleder has been granted the prestigious "Very Good" Dermatest seal of approval, as well as a "Platinum" rating in the material health category. Most tanning agents are toxic, but Olivenleder's agent is skin pH neutral, safe to eat, and nontoxic to the skin or the environment. Moreover, it improves the working conditions of people who tan and dye the material. Leather manufacturers in India, Brazil, Mexico, U.S. and Europe who have implemented the standards have reported fewer detrimental health effects among their workers, and better overall working conditions. "As we don't have any heavy metals in there, [and] also no synthetic tanning agents, it is much healthier", Lamparter explains. "For the first time, you can say it's a healthy way of tanning". Olivenleder also contains very strong antioxidants, four times stronger than those found in Vitamin C. These antioxidants are much better at preventing the decolouring effect of leather's fatliquour oxidation than conventional tanning techniques.

## USING OLIVENLEDER

Feedback on Olivenleder's quality has been positive so far. Customers are amazed at Olivenleder's wide range of colours, soft texture and pleasing appearance. The brand offers colours encompassing all shades of the spectrum: white, black, intense primary colours and even pastel shades. In "classical vegetable tanning, you normally cannot find a bright red or a bright yellow or a bright blue. They always have some kind of earthy tone to them. But Olivenleder can [make it possible], as the [base] colour is very light already", Lamparter says. The quality of the leather is equal, or superior, to the leather produced by conventional tanning processes in all but one trait: water resistance. For the most effective water resistance, like that required of army boots, chrome tanning is still the most effective process, he says. The German automotive industry has been one of the first to embrace Olivenleder's potential, with big-name clients like BMW, and now Porsche, using the leather for the upholstery and interior of the newest electric cars, like the BMW i3, the BMW i8 and the Porsche Taycan. In the past, vegetable-tanned leather was difficult to use for car upholstery due to the flexibility of the material and aesthetic problems caused by it shrinking on instrument and door panels. Due to the cross-linking of its fibre structure by the tanning agent, this is no longer an issue with Olivenleder. Industries like the automotive sector are very carefully considering their new product design to stay relevant, ensuring they are in line with the newest realities of customer's lives, and the social, economic and environmental changes that will occur in the future. It's very clear that in the next five to ten years, we will experience a range of products made with the newest, most innovative alternative materials. Hugo Boss has accepted the challenge to innovate by implementing Olivenleder in its autumn-winter 2019 line, hopefully acting as an accelerator for other European and global fashion brands. Wet-green wants to keep expanding into the fashion industry, though it is currently at the beginning of its transitional journey, taking time to evaluate and implement new material solutions. Although prices today still range between 10 to 30 percent more than conventional leather, depending on its type and thickness, many customers and tanneries are willing to implement Olivenleder for its environmental benefits. The future of the leather industry overall will most likely shift from chrome tanning in favour of sustainable methods like Olivenleder. Once sustainable leather becomes the norm, and not the exception, the production cost of Olivenleder and other sustainable brands will surely decrease as orders increase, Lamparter says. "The market is changing at the moment, becoming more transparent — and transparency is what we like", Lamparter tells us. He sees big potential markets in countries like India, Pakistan and Bangladesh – much more than in Europe. "There is a much bigger drive. They have no choice but to change", he continues. "They will already be one or two steps ahead of us in a short amount of time".

▶ **CARE ADVICE**

Like all other leathers, Olivenleder requires attentive care to retain its pristine condition and maximum durability, and extend its lifespan. Leather must be stored away from hot, dry conditions and direct light sources, as these will dry out the leather's interior oils, potentially leading to discolouration and cracking. To better preserve leather, it should be stored in breathable dust bags at a constant humidity level and should be dusted and cleaned regularly using pH-balanced soap. While excessive moisture will damage leather products — especially those made with vegetable-tanned leather — using special leather conditioners and balsams once a month will greatly enhance the look and lifespan of leather garments. Experts also recommend cleaning it with a damp washcloth after every use and washing articles of clothing by hand.

# A NEW KIND OF LEATHER TEXTILE

What's the first thing that pops into your head when you imagine garments made from jelly? It's tempting to picture bags made out of the popular wobbly dessert, but in reality, they look nothing like that. Thanks to Gelatex, a new sustainable textile, clothes made of gelatine look and feel a lot like a material we all know and love: leather.

When Mari-Ann Meigo Fonseca, Co-founder and CEO of Gelatex, began her MBA at the University of Tartu in 2016, her passion for eco-textiles led her to join a team of material scientists who were developing gelatine textiles for use in the medical industry. The dedicated scientists were quick to realize how their research could be applied to other industries, especially to fashion, and began developing the formula for a ground-breaking, gelatine-based textile. In autumn of that year, the Estonian-based team presented their first prototype of Gelatex at ClimateLaunchpad, a worldwide green business idea competition — and won. Three years later, the gelatine-based material is approaching its final testing rounds in the hopes that by 2020, it will be ready to inspire consumers all around the world. Gelatex looks to solve the age-old dilemma surrounding conventional leather production: cost-effective options, such as chrome-tanned leather, are extremely toxic for the environment, but sustainable options, such as most vegetable-tanned leathers, are expensive and take long to produce. Enter Gelatex, an affordable option that can be mass produced, is not toxic, requires no tanning process and greatly reduces waste throughout its production — opening the door to a world of accessible sustainable leather. "The idea is really to make a material that is chemically identical to leather but [is] completely eco-friendly and affordable", Meigo Fonseca tells us as she shares Gelatex's vision. The material's novelty provides a perfect platform for designers who would like to extend beyond their comfort zones and push the margins of the conventional. Gelatex wants to focus on mass production, because "in order to really [...] impact [...] the world, the solutions have to be competitive [...] compared to the non-eco solutions — price-wise and also production capacity-wise", Meigo Fonseca explains.

## PRODUCTION JOURNEY

Although Gelatex is based in Estonia, the material's journey begins in Germany, where animal waste, like skin, bones and tendons, are transformed into gelatine. According to Gelatex, more than 25 percent of animal waste from the meat industry is burned or discarded in Europe alone, adding a heavy load to global carbon emissions. All the gelatine used in Gelatex is sourced from that same material waste, enabling people to use up to five times more material per animal and providing "huge potential to actually give value to this waste", she says.

The gelatine then travels to Estonia, where it is treated with a solution comprised of many non-toxic substances to create nano- and micro-gelatine fibres which are used to create a mesh-like material. The mesh is then heated and glucose is slowly added as a cross-linker to make the material water-resistant. Then the material is pressed and a light lining made of organic, unbleached cotton is placed between two layers of gelatine fibres to increase its durability. With a final flourish, the textile is polished with natural oils for increased water resistance and rolled up ready to be distributed. Meigo Fonseca hopes that the process will become so streamlined and efficient that it will evolve into one fully automated line that reduces energy and water consumption. Gelatex's formula strives to be different from conventional leather processing in every way — especially in terms of dyeing. Researchers are still working to find the most effective ways to dye the textile, but the preliminary results are incredibly encouraging, especially in the use of natural dyes. While conventional leather needs to be dyed after tanning, sometimes with toxic substances, Gelatex is dyed before the material even begins to take shape. Pigments are added to the Gelatex solution before it turns into a fibrous mesh, resulting in a fully dyed material. "The advantage is that the material is truly coloured — all the fibres contain the pigment. The colour doesn't fade that easily", Meigo Fonseca tells us.

Photo: Mari-Ann Meigo Fonseca

## VALUE OF THE FABRIC

The main value of Gelatex for designers lies in its amazing versatility. Since the fabric is produced like a synthetic material, most of its physical characteristics are entirely controllable, including the texture, quality, density and water resistance level. Samples developed during a rigorous trial period are a great example of Gelatex's adaptability. "There are some that are more similar to leather, some that are more similar to paper, and some that are more similar to cork", describes Meigo Fonseca. She explains that the material's texture would be perfect for designing anything from car upholstery and jackets to bags and accessories.

Betting on Gelatex also means a bigger bang for your buck, as the ground-breaking technology allows for the material to be produced in rolls rather than individual hides — saving between 15 to 20 percent of material waste. Looking for even more reasons to try Gelatex? Its non-toxic nature and organic origins mean that it's biodegradable and compostable, so your clothes won't further burden the environment once you discard them.

Scientists are perfecting the leather alternative's mechanical properties, such as its endurance and flexibility and working on the final touches to ensure maximum quality. As of now, Gelatex's breathability and sweat-wicking characteristics distinguish it as a new kind of leather textile that can create its own space among existing leather products on the market. There is no doubt that the textile will develop the full capacity to compete with natural and faux leathers. Although "at the moment we can't say it's better than leather", as Meigo Fonseca explains, when you compare Gelatex to natural leather, it can be much lighter, meaning more comfort for users.

Gelatex Technologies has already been contacted by multiple leaders in the fashion industry and is looking for big partners to launch a first "capsule collection" to enter the market *en force* with. The company is also looking to collaborate closely with smaller designers and brands to form meaningful partnerships in which it can keep testing the limits of what the material can do. Generally, markets have reacted positively to Gelatex, but is it truly a material for everyone? Meigo Fonseca acknowledges that there may be some pushback from vegans, as the material is made from animal waste, but stresses that Gelatex isn't trying to be an alternative, not a substitute. She has found, however, that some vegans are very supportive of the initiative, understanding that other people eat meat and that it's beneficial to use the byproducts of this industry. "It's understandable, [...] not all the products are for everybody", she says.

The future holds endless possibilities for the leather industry, and Gelatex seems like one of the most promising. Meigo Fonseca thinks that most other eco-friendly solutions tend to be niche, expensive ones that are only accessible to "eco-enthusiasts", which is a misguided way to try to change the industry. Instead, she believes that science should keep looking for low cost, scalable eco-solutions, like Gelatex, that can make sustainability available to every budget.

*"More than 25 percent of animal waste from the meat industry is burned or discarded in Europe alone, adding a heavy load to global carbon emissions".*

▶ **CARE ADVICE**

Gelatex has not yet been released to the public, and care instructions are still liable to change. As with all new garments, you should ensure you read the item's specific care instructions. There are, however, some general guidelines you should follow when caring for leather products. Try to keep your Gelatex away from excessive heat and direct sunlight to avoid possible discolouration. Keeping your product well protected when you're not using it by covering it in a breathable dust bag is also a good rule of thumb. Be careful when using washer-dryer machines, as the wrong cycle could damage your product. If possible, hand wash and air dry your products for maximum durability.

# ENVIRONMENTAL IMPACT*

## ELECTRICITY (kWh)

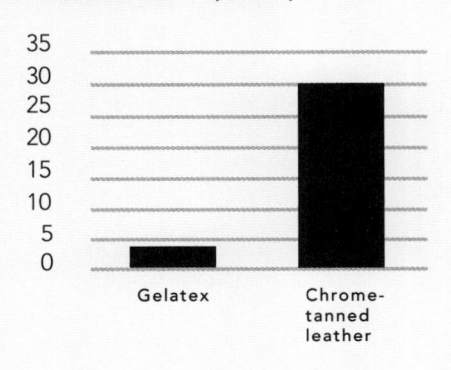

| | Gelatex | Chrome-tanned leather |
|---|---|---|
| kWh | ~3 | ~29 |

## WATER CONSUMPTION (L)

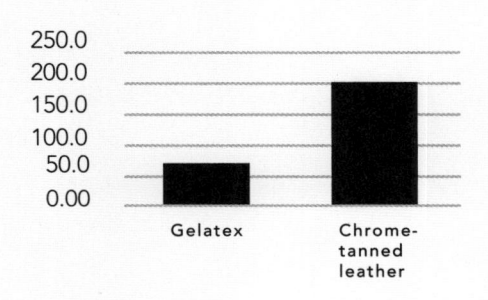

| | Gelatex | Chrome-tanned leather |
|---|---|---|
| L | ~60 | ~190 |

## CO₂ EMISSION (KG)

| | Gelatex | Chrome-tanned leather |
|---|---|---|
| kg | ~2.5 | ~21 |

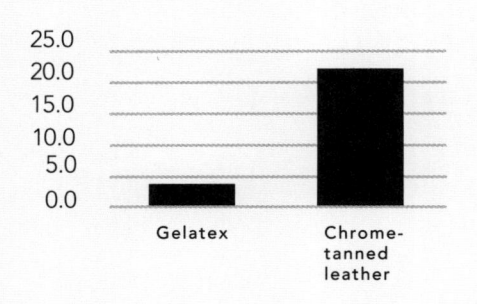

## TOXIC CHEMICALS USED (G)

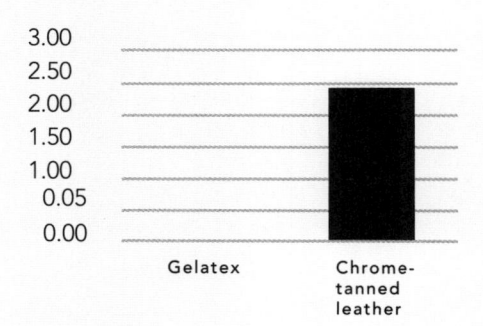

| | Gelatex | Chrome-tanned leather |
|---|---|---|
| g | 0 | ~2.25 |

*Environmental impact of Gelatex vs. Chrome-tanned leather (Calculations are made for comparing the production of 1 m² of material (weighs roughly 1kg)

# 5. SYNTHETIC FIBRES

## MICROPLASTICS

There's a good chance you've eaten plastic for dinner – and that washing your clothes was partly to blame. From the first moment you throw that brand-new polyester shirt in the washing machine it begins to release its fibres. During its journey, polyester, which is petroleum-based, breaks down to form microscopic plastic particles called microplastics. The freed fibres flow down the machine's drainage system, through sewage treatment plants and eventually into the ocean, where they are ingested by plankton, fish, shellfish, and other marine animals that are then served for dinner in households around the world.

Research shows that humans use over 240 million tons of plastic each year, much of which is not biodegradable, not recycled, and left to accumulate in waste dumps around the world. 60 to 80 percent of the litter found in European oceans is plastic, which does not biodegrade but rather breaks down into microplastics. Raffaella Mossotti, a researcher for the EU-funded **MERMAIDS** project, has studied these molecules extensively and found that around 35 percent of microplastics in the ocean come from synthetic fibres released when clothes are washed in domestic and industrial washing machines. The particles are so small – measuring less than 5 millimetres – that machine filters and sewage treatments cannot catch them or stop them from flowing down the drains directly into rivers and oceans, Mossotti explains.

Plastic is hydrophobic, making it a perfect vector for toxic substances. It has a great affinity for "persistent, bio-accumulative and toxic substances", such as polycyclic aromatic hydrocarbons, persistent organic pollutants like PCBs and DDTs, and heavy metals, the researcher says. When it decomposes into microplastic particles, the surface area increases, acting like a sponge and linking all these toxic substances together, making it an eco-toxicological problem. "Laboratory studies indicate that ingestion could cause harmful

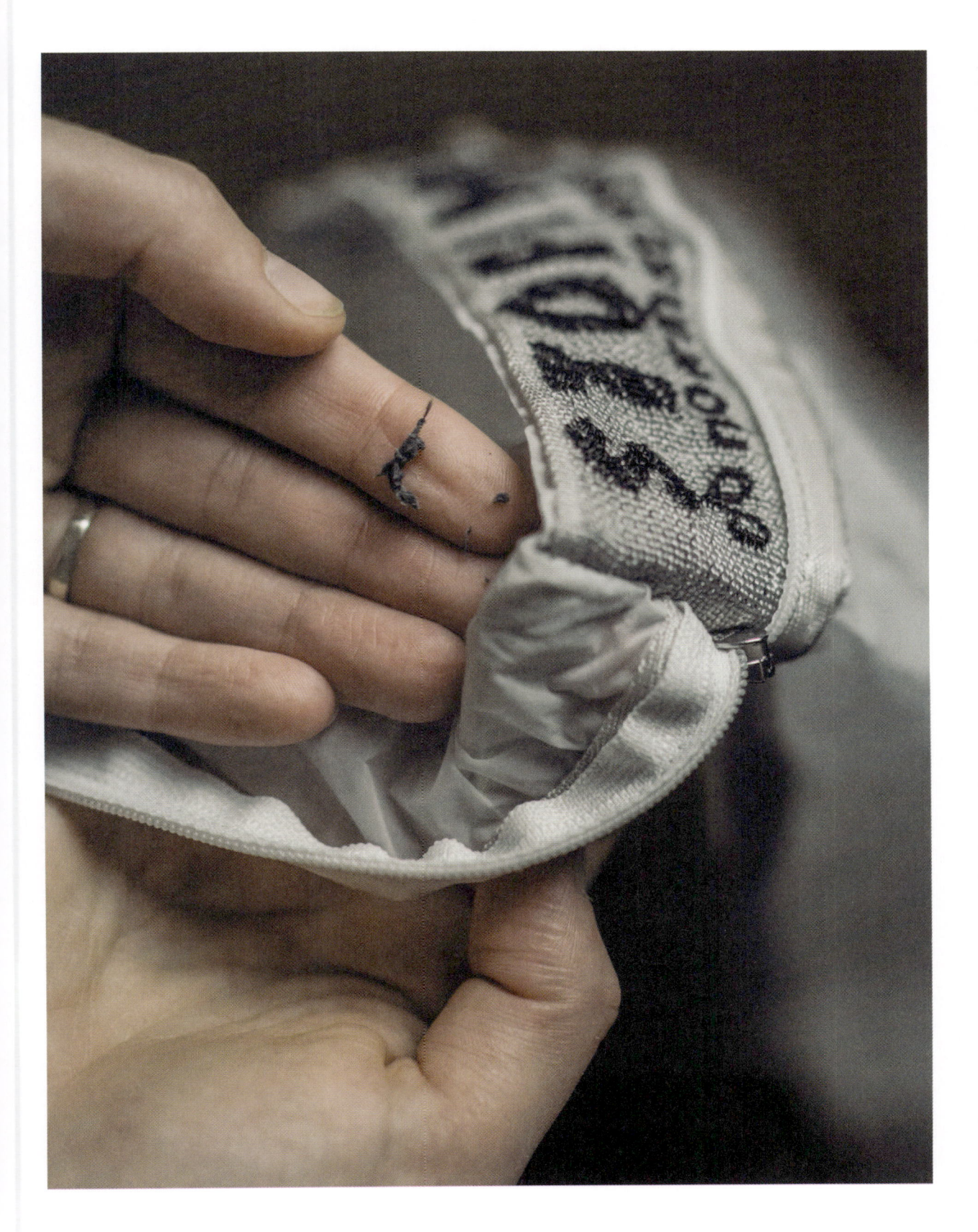

toxicological and/or physical effects", Mossotti warns, but scientists have not reached final conclusions on what these are, especially on human beings.

## THE ROLE OF SYNTHETICS

All fibres undergo significant mechanical and chemical stress when garments are washed in conventional washing machines, leading to pilling and fibre release. In the 2011 study that first brought attention to the microplastic problem, researcher Mark Browne discovered that a single garment can release over 1,900 fibres per wash. Bio-based fibres, like cotton and viscose, easily decompose and pose no threat to the environment, but petroleum-based synthetics, like polyester, polyamide, and acrylic, break down into dangerous non-biodegradable microplastics.

The biggest culprits are clothes made of polyester, as this petroleum-based fibre — hailed for its versatility and cost-effectiveness — is one of the most common microplastics found in oceans worldwide, Mossotti says. It's not that polyester textiles release more fibres than other synthetic fibres, she clarifies, but rather that we use higher quantities of it — in 2018, polyester accounted for three-quarters of the 71.6 million tons of man-made fibres. Mossotti has conducted most of her research using polyester fibres because the sheer volume of their microplastics floating in our oceans currently pose the biggest threat to ecosystems. Many people have hailed recycled polyester as the hope for the future. It is eco-friendly, reduces waste and carbon dioxide emissions, and can be recycled up to three times. In the end, however, even recycled PET is still PET. "It's the same fibre — the release doesn't depend on the polyester polymer, but on the structure of the yarn, fibres (either single filament or stapled) and structure of the fabric (woven or knitted)", Mossotti says. Although no new plastic is being produced, recycled polyester garments can release the same number of fibres as virgin polyester textiles.

## WHAT CAUSES FIBRE RELEASE?

The experiments Mossotti did for the MERMAIDS project shed a lot of light on the factors that influence the amount of microplastic produced when clothes are washed. The team of researchers quantified the microplastics released from polyester garments under different washing conditions, changing everything from the temperature of the water and number of times the load was centrifuged to the types of detergent used. They also altered the fabric type and textile processes. Based on these experiments, Mossotti and her team concluded that the amount of microplastics a fibre produces depends on eight factors: fibre length, yarn twist, linear density, or yarn count, fabric density, textile geometry and pilling propensity, washing conditions, and stitching.

***Fibre length:*** Shorter fibres increase the chance of fibres migrating to the textile's surface, increasing pilling and microfibre release.
***Yarn twist:*** Twisted yarns are more resistant and elastic, producing compact yarns that shed less.
***Linear density:*** Thicker fabrics have more fibres, so they shed more.
***Fabric density:*** Denser fabrics create tighter structures and decrease the probability of shedding.
***Textile geometry and pilling propensity:*** There are different types of textile construction, from knits to woven fabrics, that influence fibre release. Knitted fabrics and those that pill more release more fibres.
***Washing conditions:*** Water temperature, bath ratio, type and pH of detergent, and time influence shedding.
***Stitching:*** Textiles can be stitched in two ways: polyester or welded. Polyester stitching is generally used as it is stronger and more resistant. However, depending on washing conditions, this may cause further release of microplastics.

Textile geometry is one of the most important factors determining microplastic release, Mossotti argues. Synthetic fibres are created through a polymerisation process that allows the product to be manipulated and shaped in many ways. They can be long, short, twisted together or left single, and this difference in construction affects fibre release. "Other important factors are the operative washing conditions, because, for example, the same textiles washed in different washing cycles release in different ways", Mossotti says. Powder detergents, basic detergents, and power oxidizing agents increase fibre release, as do higher water temperatures, high-speed centrifugation, and washing cycles with a high number of rinses, she continues. These factors exert more stress on the garments and fibres, leading to more discharge. Ultimately, the interaction between textile construction and washing conditions determine the number of microfibres released – the more interaction garments have with washing materials, the likelier a garment will release fibres. After the MERMAIDS project, three companies asked Mossotti's team to quantify how many microplastics their fabric production was releasing to understand how to improve their production cycle. Aquafil, a major yarn producer, depolymerizes polyamides coming from discarded fishing nets to develop a line of recycled nylon fibres called ECONYL. They have joined forces with Mossotti's lab as they implement the researcher's quantification method. "The level of sensitization to environmental problems is high", she says about the collaboration.

## SOLUTIONS

"It's not possible to eliminate all the polyester in fabrics, because no other fibres can replace it", Mossotti states. Regardless, there are various ways consumers, manufactures and designers can collaborate to mitigate the fibre's effects on the environment. She believes that the first step is to encourage eco-designs when producing garments while simultaneously furthering research into bio-based, degradable synthetic fibres. In the future, she hopes that European research labs will find a way to standardize microplastic quantification methods, because currently the lack of these makes it difficult to compare results and come to a consensus on the best way to approach microplastics.

In Mossotti's opinion, the most effective solution would be installing filters on washing machines that can catch microfibres as they are released, but there are still limited options available on the market. During her experiments. Mossotti used a prototype filter but found it too difficult to use because the high number of fibres released clogged the filter quickly and needed replacing after 20 washes. A Slovenian company, called Planet Care Solutions, sells filters that can last up to 20 washes. According to their website, "Independent tests have confirmed this showing a marked reduction in the release of even the smallest particles down to 5 micrometres (the thickness of fibres is normally between 10 – 20 micrometres)". The company is working with suppliers to make washing machines with pre-installed filters, but they are still not available for purchase.

▶ **CARE ADVICE**

In the meantime, there are 10 steps you can follow to reduce synthetic garments' wear and tear when doing the laundry. Ten for the Ocean is an initiative started by STOP! Micro Waste, a non-profit organization dedicated to limiting the spread of microplastics in the environment.

### Step 1: Skip Plastics
Buy fewer garments made of synthetic textiles, opting instead for better quality, microfibre-free alternatives.

### Step 2: Stay Cool
Wash your clothes with cooler water; coloureds at 40°C and bed linen at 60°C. Mossotti also strongly recommends always keeping the water temperature under 40°C.

### Step 3: Wash Less
Air your clothes out and remove stains by hand instead of throwing them into the washer.

### Step 4: Skip Spin Cycle
Spinning increases friction between clothes, leading to more fibre release. Reduce the rotations per minute, or skip spinning altogether.

### Step 5: Separate Solids
Don't wash your clothes along with any solid materials, like shoes, shin guards, washing balls or soap nuts. These exert a lot of mechanical pressure on clothes leading to fibre breakage.

### Step 6: Hard vs. Soft
Before doing your laundry, separate textiles into two groups: hard and soft surfaces. Hard textiles can rub on softer ones, creating more friction.

### Step 7: Air-Dry Synthetics
Exposing synthetics to the heat and mechanical forces inside tumble dryers can lead to more fibre release.

Photo: Stop! Micro Waste

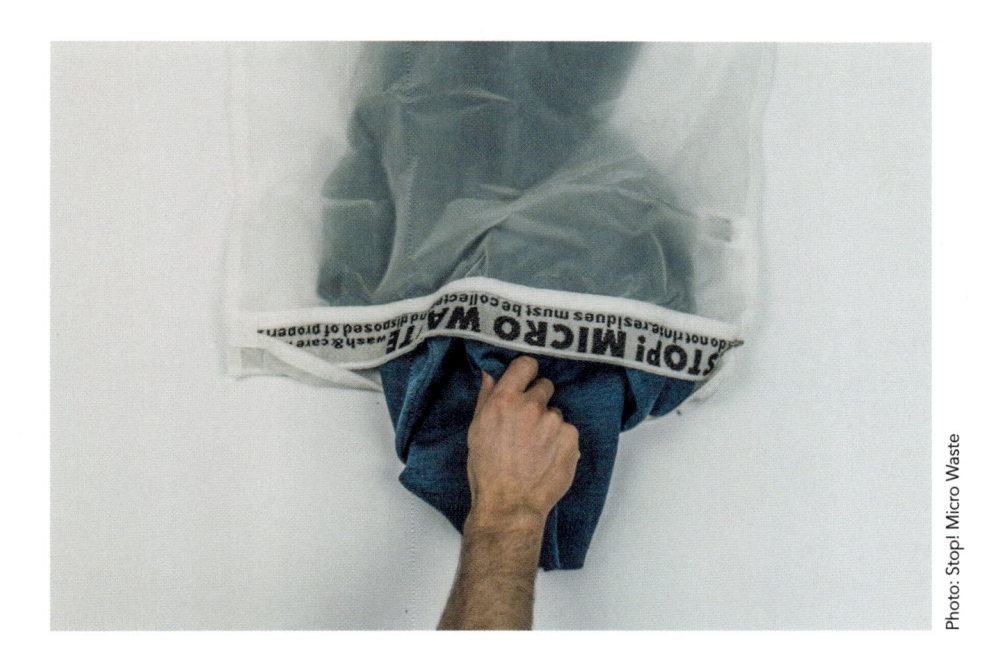

### Step 8: Shorten Cycle Step
Longer washing times increase clothes friction and fibre breakage.

### Step 9: Better Detergents
Choose liquid detergents over powdered ones, Mossotti recommends, because powder detergents can be abrasive to textile surfaces. She also suggests using more softeners and detergents with neutral pH values.

### Step 10: Use a filter
Build or buy a filter for your dryer's wastewater or buy STOP! Micro waste's special washing bag, called Guppyfriend. It was invented to prevent breakage and catch synthetic fibres before they can make their way into the ocean.

# AFTERWORD

What a journey from Asia to Europe! Now you can breathe, drink some olive tea and decide who you want to be. The choice is only yours, coming from your heart! If you found yourself inspired by designers, experts and textile stories, then invest your precious time in the right direction for an innovative fashion future, full of surprises, experiments and unknown results. Now you are well-versed in fashion jargon!

We wanted to awaken your inner rooted values on life and fashion which remain priceless. No matter if you are a global citizen or a villager, we believe in the power of information received at the right time of one's life and from knowledgeable people who may inspire or lead the search for future answers. If somebody gets addicted to finding the truth, time is the only limit.

# LIST OF CONTRIBUTORS

Stefano Lupicano, Smart Artist; Anna Gallucci Colling, The University of Kent; Earl Singh, Fashion for Good; Thimo Schwenzfeier, Messe Frankfurt Exhibition GmbH; Ishwari Thopte, Center for Fashion Enterprise; Andrea Rosso, MYAR srl; Elin Larsson, Elco; Julia Pettersson, Filippa K AB; Bert van Son, MUD Jeans International B.V.; Amit Jain, Funky Kalakar Private Limited; Elsien Gringhuis, Studio Elsien Gringhuis; Eva Power, The Ethical Silk Company; Katia Nicolas, Good Krama; Grace Huam, Graciela Huam; Cecília Silva, Tavira Flagship Shop. Koziishop, Lda; Heather Kaye, Golden Finch Trading (Shanghai) Co. Ltd; Marita Setas Ferro, Marita Setas Unipessoal Lda; Sebastian Thies, nat-2™. K&T Handels- und Unternehmensberatung GmbH; Rae Indah-Purnama, Purnama outreach Pte Ltd; Wan Tseng, WISP Ltd; Brands: La feme MiMi, Kozii, Benedetti Life, Plant Faced Clothing, Grand Step Shoes, Lucy & Yak, IMRECZEOVA, MonCinta, JAN 'N JUNE; Sandy MacLennan, East Central Studios Ltd; David Shah, View Publications; Santi Mallorquí Gou, Organic Cotton Colours; Pauline Guesné, INDUO; Jeroen Muijsers, Flocus BV; Camilla Carrara. Ana Tavares, Tintex Textiles, S.A.; Marie Demaegdt, Alain Camilleri, CELC Developpement; Ing. Christoph Kobler, Leinenweberei Vieböck GmbH; Chandra Prakash Jha, Cocccon UG; Paqui Ferrer, Hilaturas Ferre, S.A.; Angela Zen, Panama Trimmings srl; Thomas Lamparter, wet-green GmbH; Mari-Ann Meigo Fonesca, Gelatex Technologies OÜ; Alberto Rossi, Chargeurs Wool Sales Europe Srl; Dr.ssa Raffaella Mossotti, CNR ISMAC; Julia Krippendorf, STOP! Micro Waste.